To Liz—

I hope Dad's story

A Good Man

REDISCOVERING
MY FATHER,
SARGENT SHRIVER

---

of faith, hope and love brings

Mark K. Shriver

you much JOY -- And a few challenges, too!

Mark K Shriver

🦁 ST. MARTIN'S GRIFFIN 🦋 NEW YORK

www.stmartins.com

The Library of Congress has cataloged the Henry Holt edition as follows:

Shriver, Mark K. (Mark Kennedy), 1964–
  A good man : rediscovering my father, Sargent Shriver /
Mark K. Shriver.—1st ed.
    p.   cm.
  ISBN 978-0-8050-9544-9 (hardcover)
  ISBN 978-0-8050-9532-6 (e-book)
  1. Shriver, Sargent, 1915–2011.   2. Shriver, Sargent, 1915–2011—
Philosophy.   3. Shriver, Sargent, 1915–2011—Influence.   4. Shriver,
Sargent, 1915–2011—Family.   5. Shriver, Mark K. (Mark Kennedy),
1964–   6. Shriver, Mark K. (Mark Kennedy), 1964– —Family.   7. Father
and sons—United States.   8. Fathers—United States—Biography.
9. Politicians—United States—Biography.   I. Title.
  E840.8.S525 S35 2012
  973.924092—dc23
  [B]

                                                        2011050028

        ISBN 978-1-250-03144-0 (trade paperback)

St. Martin's Griffin books may be purchased for educational, business, or promotional use. For information on bulk purchases, please contact Macmillan Corporate and Premium Sales Department at 1-800-221-7945 extension 5442 or write specialmarkets@macmillan.com.

First published in hardcover by Henry Holt and Company

First St. Martin's Griffin Edition: May 2013

D 10 9 8 7 6 5 4

For Molly, Tommy, and Emma, and for

CONTENTS

A Good Man

INTRODUCTION

I was anxious and my heart was pounding as Dad and I drove east on Route 50 toward the Chesapeake Bay. We were running late—not unheard of in my family but unacceptable to the hunting guides of Maryland's Eastern Shore, who always insisted on a predawn rendezvous. Dad was doing his best to make up for lost time by obliterating the speed limit, but we were still behind. As we slowed to pay the toll, I could feel the cool autumn air and already see the streaks of sunrise on the horizon—and we still had forty minutes to go.

These hunting trips were a ritual for us, but my postcollege life—a new job, new commitments, maybe even new priorities—was starting to disrupt the regularity of our father-son reunions. And as the hum from the tires changed pitch when we began to cross the giant steel bridge that traverses the Chesapeake, I grew more irritated with Dad.

He knew that I was working grueling hours at a nonprofit I'd started in Baltimore and that it was hard for me to get away from those responsibilities. And as a lifelong hunter and Marylander, he knew the birds started moving early, and was well aware of the guides' protocol. Nonetheless, he'd been close to a half hour late.

We ascended the bridge's incline in silence, I quietly stewing and Dad lost in his own thoughts. By the time we got to the midway point of the four-mile-long steel structure, the full expanse of the choppy bay below and the low-lying shore ahead were beginning to be illuminated by the morning sun.

The birds will already be flying, I thought to myself. I was growing more annoyed just as Dad, staring out at the same daybreak, suddenly broke the silence, his thoughts far from that day's hunt. "Look at *that!*" he cried, awestruck. "I can't wait to meet God. I can't wait to meet the Creator who made such a beautiful sunrise!"

Staring out the side window I mumbled a sarcastic response: "Yeah, it's beautiful, Dad. Thanks for pointing it out."

Moments later, as we reached the final expanse of the bridge, it felt as if we were driving straight into the rising sun, massive and reddish yellow over the Eastern Shore, waiting to swallow us up at the end of our crossing.

I looked over at Dad, his face awash in the bright light. He was staring straight into the sun in a state of awe, eyes wide and unblinking. I could tell he was repeating to himself over and over what he'd just exclaimed aloud: *I can't wait to meet the Creator who made such a beautiful sunrise . . . I can't wait to meet God . . .*

We finally made it to the ragged cornfield, a bit behind schedule but not so late as to cause any real problems. Dad was in a typically buoyant mood all morning. He chatted incessantly with our two guides in the goose blind, asking about their lives and families and cracking jokes and becoming fast friends in no time, as only he could. And when the geese finally came in close, he couldn't contain his excitement, and he whooped and cheered us on—causing the first gaggle we saw to reverse course and fly off to safety.

Our attempts to get him to shush fell on deaf ears. He

kept talking and laughing, at one point breaking out a Snickers bar, taking a hearty bite, and sincerely reacting as if it were a rare delicacy. "This is absolutely terrific!" he half-whispered. "Who wants to try a bite?!" Our guides shook with laughter, which only made his smile broader.

Somehow we managed, despite Dad's antics, to get a few geese that morning. I don't think Dad pulled the trigger once, though, preferring instead to watch and congratulate everyone else with a slap on the back. "My God!" he'd shout. "What a fantastic shot! You are a magnificent waterfowl hunter!" His mood was contagious, and everyone—me included—had a wonderful time.

But I was still anxious. No longer because of his late arrival but because of a contradiction I'd never been able to figure out about my father, one that had been demonstrated to me so starkly in the span of a few hours. His infectious cheer that morning stood in glaring contrast to his startling comment on the bridge earlier: "I can't wait to meet God." I knew Dad's faith was unshakable, that he went to daily Mass without fail, and that his great loves in life were God and my mom. But how could someone so full of life be so ready for death? Not fearful of it but almost longing for it? How could he, quite literally, be excited to die?

He was seventy-three, but you'd never know it. He possessed the energy of a teenager, he looked half his age, and his remarkably full and active life had shown no sign of slowing down. As he had throughout so much of his life, he was getting important things done—still traveling the world, meeting prime ministers and presidents, working tirelessly and effectively to open the doors of freedom and opportunity for people who had historically been denied those things. He was constantly surrounded by his children and their growing families, he was more helplessly in love with his wife of thirty-five years than ever before, and everywhere he went he saw old friends and made new ones. He had his health, financial security, and, at this point in his life, the freedom and ability to do whatever he chose.

And yet he could stare into the sun and tell his fourth-born child that he couldn't wait to leave it all behind. I simply couldn't balance the two extremes: why was my dad, a guy so filled with vitality, looking forward to his own death?

◇

Fast-forward twenty-two years. My mom, Eunice Kennedy Shriver, had died a year earlier, on August 11, 2009, and my dad was engaged in a heroic but losing battle with Alzheimer's. His doctor had told my siblings and me that, at ninety-four, Dad would probably not live more than another twelve to eighteen months. When we related this to Dad's lawyer, Bob Corcoran, he reminded us that, some thirty years earlier, Dad had written a letter that he'd asked Bob to hold until his death. We thought that, given all the decisions that had had to be made in a tight time frame after Mom's death, we should know whether Dad had left specific instructions about his wake, funeral, burial site, and so on.

So in August 2010, Bob sent us the letter, which landed at the family home in Hyannis Port like a stealth rocket amid the chaos of five children, four in-laws, nineteen grandchildren, and Dad himself. Everyone was running in different directions, playing tennis and baseball and sailing.

I noticed an open FedEx envelope on the counter and asked my brother Timmy whether the letter was in it. He said yes, that he'd opened it and read it, then left it for the others. I read it, quickly, and was moved by its beauty and thoughtfulness, but shortly after I finished, my kids pulled me away. I set the letter aside, determined to go back to it in more serene moments. That serenity never came.

Three months later, Dad celebrated his ninety-fifth birthday in style. We had a party for him at our house. Grandkids ran all around and took turns sitting on Dad's lap. We laughed and sang. Dad smiled and shouted out a few words of joy. He opened his presents and gobbled up his cake and ice cream. It was a great night, but he was clearly slipping. The letter crossed my mind—*I have to find a quiet time to really read it*, I thought.

The rest of November and December were jam-packed with Thanksgiving and Christmas and family visits. Work was as crazy as ever—I was running Save the Children's U.S. Programs and on the road at least two days a week, pitching prospective donors, lobbying state and federal elected officials, and seeing the kids in our programs. My own kids' sporting events consumed the weekend—we were busy doing everything we could to keep up with the Joneses.

Even though Dad lived less than three miles from us, I didn't see him as much as I wanted to, or should have, because, well, life with three kids and a wife, a job requiring lots of travel, and other commitments spread me too thin. And there was, of course, Alzheimer's. For almost ten years I'd been in charge of Dad's finances and medical care. Each small step in his decline became another devastation for me, from taking away his car keys to hiring an assistant and then full-time providers; from explaining Mom's death to him to moving him out of their home. Our visits together could still be enchanting, especially when my kids were with me, but it was painful to see the brightest, most inquisitive, most joyful person I knew struggle to piece together short sentences. When Dad smiled and told the kids or me that he loved us or that we were wonderful, it made me happy—but it also made me miss him even more.

So, in early January, as I packed for a flight to Los Angeles for a Save the Children event, I remembered to take the letter with me. Dad's doctor, on our last call, had made it pretty clear that Dad was not going to live to see ninety-six. He had just reentered the hospital for the second time in a month. I didn't think he was going to die in the next few days, but I wanted to read the letter again and jot down a few thoughts in case I had to give a eulogy.

I had a window seat, and as the plane took off from Dulles International Airport, we headed east, toward the Chesapeake Bay. I realized the pilot was following air traffic control's direction before banking south and then heading west. But he sure seemed to be taking his time doing it.

Then I looked out the window, and the memory smacked me in the face. There was the Bay Bridge, there was the hearty, glowing sun, and there were Dad and I driving that morning so many years ago.

I pulled out the letter and started to read. Maybe it was because I knew his death was so imminent, or maybe it was sitting alone in an airplane away from my family; whatever it was, the letter overwhelmed me. He had written it in 1979, at the age of sixty-four. Why would a man so relatively young and vigorous be thinking about death—telling us the mechanics of his burial, his intended preparations in heaven for Mom and even for our eventual arrivals there, his eternal love for Mom and each of us? He was thinking about these things a decade before our Bay Bridge crossing. Why would he write such a note, drenched with mortality, to his wife and five children? He'd added a P.S. to the letter in 1987, at the age of seventy-two, and said that he was still in agreement with everything he had written earlier.

I pulled out a pad and started to write. I wanted to put some thoughts on paper about my father, his eventful life, and his commitment to public service. I wanted to somehow convey who I thought he was, not just as a public man but, more importantly, as a father, husband, and friend.

Four days later, I received the long-dreaded call from

Timmy—Dad was slipping, and it was a matter of days. I had to return home from California immediately if I wanted to see him before he died.

The days leading up to his death were filled with Rosaries and Masses by his bedside, with final good-byes by all of the kids, grandkids, and in-laws. My siblings—the oldest, Bobby; my older sister and brother, Maria and Timmy; and my younger brother, Anthony—and I spent time together and started planning the wake and funeral.

The busyness of funeral planning, I hoped, would keep me from my grief for the time being. But the process itself became an education that would change my life. From encounters and discoveries over the next few days, I began to get the sense that Dad really wasn't who I thought he was— that he was far more complex and intriguing. I began to realize that the circumstances of the last ten years—including my congressional race and all the details of tending to Dad as he struggled with Alzheimer's—had kept me from exploring, let alone understanding, my father's insistent joy, powerful faith, generous spirit, and hopeful view of life.

I'd lost track of who he was, what he'd done, and what he'd said and written. He wrote me a letter almost every day of my adult life, many by hand, most typed. Some I read quickly; some I put in a file to be read later and never got back to. I had not mined all this material, which could have enriched my own outlook on life. His life was a treasure trove of moral examples and ethical inspiration, but in my hustle and bustle, I had failed to identify this spiritual guide living right before my eyes. Straying into the dark woods of ambition and self-involvement, I was losing track of the principles that defined his every day.

The letter had shaken me out of this ten-year fog—and other experiences were now following furiously.

I was tasked with picking the coffin. Dad had made this

job easier for me per the directions in his final letter—he wanted to be buried in a sack, like the Trappist monks he so admired.

When I tried to satisfy this request, I learned that the government prohibited such interment for public health reasons, but I did find that Trappist monks in Iowa were building coffins. I studied the website and chose a walnut box, finely crafted but simple. I phoned the monks to go over the details; a little while later, the director called me back and told me that he had met Dad once and would do whatever I asked. He said that it would be an honor to help because Dad was such a "good man."

Over the coming days, I heard that phrase time and again. That old cliché—"a good man"—suddenly became confounding to me. I heard it so often during the days before the funeral that it passed from a cliché to an irritant to a haunting refrain.

The phrase had been used by the Bush administration to describe Michael Brown, the head of FEMA during Hurricane Katrina, and Russian president Vladimir Putin. It had grown stale, like an old cowboy line in a spaghetti western on insomniac television.

I had lost count of the people who had applied it to Dad when they'd reached out to me. At first, I thought that the cliché was just an easy out, words for people who didn't know what else to say.

But then I realized that they were taking the phrase back. Through their repetition, if not their realization, they were redeeming words that I thought had been put out to linguistic pasture.

Some of the more startling instances came back to me as I knelt in the dark beside Dad's coffin on the morning of the funeral. A prominent U.S. senator who knew Dad well, yet obviously didn't know him as well as he thought he had, told me, "I knew your dad had done a lot, but he did much more than I had known. He was a good, good man."

Ms. Wilson and Ms. Williams, both of whom waited in the wake line at Holy Trinity Catholic Church in George-town for forty-five minutes told me that they were waitresses at Reeves Restaurant, Dad's regular lunch spot across from his office. And before that, Ms. Wilson had waited on him at the Hot Shoppes in Bethesda for thirty-five years. They wanted to tell me that they had never met a more polite, thoughtful man in their forty years of work. "He was such a good man," they said simultaneously.

I will never forget the rumble of the garbage truck out-side my house on the day of the wake and seeing Calvin, the trash collector, standing in our driveway, trying to decide whether to walk up to the front door and knock. I made it easy for him; I was on the lawn and went toward him. He had tears in his eyes. He took off his dirty gloves, wiped his palms on his work clothes, and reached out his hands for mine.

"What a life," Calvin said. "I read about your dad in the paper and, man, I had to put the paper down. I had to take a step back—whoa! He helped so many people—what a good man!"

I also couldn't shake my conversation with Edwin at the wake. He worked for US Airways and had crossed paths with Dad many times during those years of travel. Not long ago, he'd seen Dad struggling and had spent half an hour helping him get through the security line. Edwin waited in that line at the wake, too, and told me that those thirty min-utes were some of the most special ones in his life.

"I never met anyone in all my years like your father," he said. "He was such a good man."

Brad Blank, a childhood friend of mine from Cape Cod, called and told me that Dad had written him thoughtful letters a number of times over the years. He'd even discussed the Judaic Studies program at Brown with Brad, saying it surpassed courses in Christianity there.

Brad said, "Your father knew more about Judaism than I do. He was such a mensch. Do you know what that means?" Before I could respond, he blurted out, "It means your father was a good man."

Throughout the planning of the funeral, Jeannie Main, Dad's longtime assistant, was at every meeting. I asked her, finally, how long she had worked with him.

"Thirty-three years," she said. "I volunteered on the McGovern-Shriver campaign in '72 and went to work for him full-time afterward."

"That's a long time," I said.

"Yes, it is, but your dad was special," she said. "Not too many big-time lawyers would listen to their assistants. Your dad always did. He didn't always agree with me, but he always listened. He was a very good man."

We got a call from Vice President Joe Biden a few hours after Dad died. The vice president told me that he never would have won his race for Senate in 1972 had Dad not shown up on the last night and rallied a crowd that worked through the night and all Election Day. Biden won by 3,162 votes, and he credited Dad with the difference.

"He didn't have to do that for me," he said. "I was an unknown kid who wasn't expected to win. Delaware is a small state, and it was the last night of a long campaign. There wasn't much, if anything, in it for him. But that was the least of what he did for our country—he was a good, good man."

Then I thought about our kids and how, just the day before, I had watched them eat breakfast with their usual gusto. When my eleven-year-old son Tommy got up and took his plates to the sink and started washing them, I almost lost it, remembering how, two years prior, Tommy had watched Dad, Alzheimer-stricken and hobbled, grab his own cake plate after the party for his ninety-third birthday, take it to the sink, and clean it. Tommy had looked at me, licked the icing off his last forkful, and followed Dad to the sink with his plate. Tommy had observed, at a very young age, what a good man Dad was, right down to the smallest detail of etiquette.

The great man is recognized for his civic achievements. The good man can be great in that arena, too, but even greater at home, on the sidewalk, at the diner, with his grandkids, at the supermarket, at church—wherever human interaction requires integrity and compassion. Dad was good because he was great in the smaller, unseen corners of life. He insisted on greatness in every facet of the daily grind. Nowhere was this clearer than in his role as our father.

During the weeks and months after the funeral, the same sort of condolences kept piling in. The "good man" phrase kept cropping up, and I realized how important it was becoming for my own life, and perhaps for all those who wanted to know how Dad lived so well, to understand him more completely. We all loved reflecting on his life together, yet most of us—family and friends and complete strangers who had admired him from afar—were looking to solve the riddle of "Sarge" for our own sakes. We wanted some of that; we wanted to bottle his mojo for ourselves.

I received thousands of letters and e-mails—many from people I didn't know at all and many from those I knew well who, after reading about Dad or attending his funeral, opened their hearts to me. So many were struggling to balance their love of family with their work, struggling with their faith, struggling with giving back to their communities. I realized that I, too, was struggling mightily with balancing it all. What's more, I had spent far too much time and energy chasing the illusory achievements that our culture associates with being a so-called great man.

One person who attended the funeral told me that he had

never been in a church for two and a half hours but that at the end of Dad's funeral, he didn't want to leave. Most seemed to dearly want to be a good man or a good woman, and they kept asking me questions: How did your dad do it all? How could he have been happily married for fifty-six years and yet there'd never been even a rumor about his relationship with my mother? How could he have raised five children who all idolized him? Been a steadfast friend to so many men and women? How could he have created, out of nothing, the most enduring legacy of the Kennedy administration—the Peace Corps—and then, while still the head of the Peace Corps, created Lyndon Johnson's most important domestic initiative, the War on Poverty—Head Start, Job Corps, VISTA, and Legal Services, to name just a few programs? And every day he went to Mass!

This book is the story of the journey I immediately undertook—was driven to undertake—to discover how a ninety-five-year-old man who had been crushed in his two national election races (for vice president with George McGovern in 1972 and for president in 1976), who had not run for office in over thirty-five years, who had been battling Alzheimer's for ten years, nevertheless inspired countless others to live a good life.

I worked, with a relentless, consoling, and consuming need, to understand the lessons of his life and his final struggle with Alzheimer's—lessons about the durability of faith, the endurance of hope, and the steadfastness of love. How had he been so faithful? So hopeful? And so loving? These were the three guiding principles of his life—faith, hope, and love—and I needed to get to the source of them.

Most of all, I wanted to understand the riddle of his joy. I knew that his uncanny, boundless joy had powered him every day of his life. Where did it come from? How did he sustain it, gracing so many of us along the way? For my family and friends, for his admirers, and for me, I wanted to discover the source of his joy so we could all try to live the same way, so I could use him as my guide as I strove to be a better man, to be as good a man as he.

PART I

PART 1

FAITH

Inspire us with the faith that God is above us and with us and that He will help us if we will do what is right. Stir our consciences. Strengthen our will. Inspire and challenge us to take our principles into the toughest walks of life and make them work.

—Sargent Shriver, National Conference
on Religion and Race
January 15, 1963

◇

CHAPTER I

LIFE AND DEATH

My mom was one month pregnant with me when she accompanied her older brother Jack to the home country, the Republic of Ireland. Jackie Kennedy was under doctor's orders not to go on the trip with her husband. She, too, was pregnant but had been put on bed rest. Mom didn't tell anyone that she was pregnant, for fear of missing the trip of a lifetime—the first Irish Catholic president visiting the family homeland, and Mom playing the role of First Lady! Nothing was going to hold her back from going to Ireland. The crowds were raucous everywhere they went—as if a long-suffering people had shed the curse of centuries of poverty to occupy the White House right along with Ireland's most famous export.

But the joy felt on this trip would not last long—just two months later, the First Family's two-day-old son, Patrick, died. Ireland and America grieved.

I obviously had no idea of the additional drama I was soon to be born into. Surely a magical realist writer like Gabriel García Márquez could have plumbed the narrative possibility of telling the story of Jack's assassination from the perspective of a baby inside the womb of the dead president's sister. The details I would have witnessed from that privileged perch: On Friday, November 22, Mom called Dad from the obstetrician's office to see if he could sneak out of the Peace Corps office for lunch with her and my soon-to-be older brother Timmy. They waited for him at a table in the dining room at the Hotel Lafayette. She was pregnant at age forty-two, but with her strong jawline and few wrinkles, she looked thirty and had the energy of a twenty-something. She would go on to have my brother Anthony at forty-four, and she dared, contrary to the tenets of medicine and the culture, to get pregnant again at forty-six, albeit losing the baby in a miscarriage.

No doubt she was happy that day, doubly so as Dad entered the room and smiled at her because he already knew the appointment had gone well. They didn't know yet that a boy would follow Bobby, Maria, and Timmy—they waited for that to reveal itself the old-fashioned way.

After a little while, the waiter came over to the table and told Dad that he had an urgent call from his assistant.

As Dad walked back to the table, Mom, I assume, could detect the change in his demeanor. He surely wasn't smiling; I suppose he was staring at her, studying her, and that his whole gait and facial expression had grown grave.

He sat down, and must have run through the consequences of what he was about to tell her: How would it affect the health of a woman whose beloved father had had a debilitating stroke? Whose oldest brother, Joe, had been killed in World War II when his plane exploded over England on a secret mission? Whose older sister had died in an airplane crash in France shortly after the war? How would the news affect the health of that baby—me—whom he saw as a sacred gift from God?

He surely collected himself, soothing her eyes with his. He spoke softly and assuredly, somehow making slightly bearable the incomprehensible news that her brother had been shot.

They left the restaurant and headed to the Peace Corps building, where a wire flash announced that Jack had died. Mom and Dad and a few Peace Corps staffers knelt and prayed in Dad's office. More reports poured in, confirming the news. Dad called a quick staff meeting and decided to send a wire to Peace Corps staff around the world, informing them of what had happened and reassuring them that the Peace Corps would continue its work.

Dad asked his assistant, Mary Ann Orlando, to take Timmy and gather my other future siblings together at our home in Rockville, while Mom and he went to the White House. There they met with both Uncle Bobby and Uncle Teddy and decided that Mom and Teddy would go to Massachusetts to be with their mother and father, and Bobby would go to Andrews Air Force Base, in Maryland, to meet the arrival of Air Force One. Dad was ostensibly in charge at the White House.

Hours later, Jackie Kennedy sent word that she wanted Dad to lead the planning of the funeral.

Soon after that, he learned that the mutual disdain between Bobby and the new president, Lyndon Johnson, threatened the smoothness of the transition and the basic functioning of the government. And he, a soon-to-be father (again) whose greatest preoccupation had been the health of his wife, was one of the few people who could bridge the gap and help the stunned country maintain its footing.

For the next few days he slept just an hour a night; he stopped working only to make his frequent calls to Mom to bolster her. He grasped the national craving for a funeral unlike any other—stately yet healing, official yet personal.

Were García Márquez telling the story, he would have shown how a steady father began to radiate his faith and hope and love to his unborn son, sparking my lifelong devotion to him.

Fiction aside, I firmly believe that Dad's faith in God gave him the strength and the discipline to orchestrate the funeral events—at times grisly, at times heartbreaking, by turns wrapped in ambition, intrigue, chaos, pathos, and raw grief.

Jackie had requested that Uncle Jack lie in state in the East Room of the White House, as had President Lincoln, and that the room be made over to look as it had then. Dad immediately called upon Jack's favorite artist, Bill Walton, to handle this assignment. Together they decided that to replicate exactly the appearance of the White House after President Lincoln's death, as requested, was impossible because of the physical changes inside the building since then. They did, however, drape black crepe over much of the East Room. Since the White House had no exterior lighting, Dad worked through the night to arrange for hand-lit torches to line the driveway. At three-thirty on Saturday morning, the Washington highway department delivered the torches, creating a scene that was seared in the nation's memory.

At just that time, Dad realized that there were no military personnel at the White House to form an honor guard that would act as an escort for Uncle Jack's arrival. Dad told a White House aide to call the marine barracks in D.C. and request men in full dress uniform. Within twenty minutes, twelve men from the Marine Silent Drill Platoon had been roused out of the barracks and, in full dress uniform, appeared at the White House.

When Jackie and the coffin arrived just a few minutes later, at four-thirty A.M., Dad stood at the doorway to greet her and direct the military pallbearers.

There were countless other decisions to be made, some immediately but all within the incredibly short time frame of three days: whom to invite to the funeral and where, mindful of protocol, to seat each person; where President

Kennedy should be buried, and whether he should lie in state in an open or a closed casket.

Dad worked with Richard Cardinal Cushing of Boston and Archbishop Patrick O'Boyle of Washington, D.C., to iron out the details of the funeral Mass at St. Matthew's Cathedral. The church leaders wanted a High Mass, but Dad convinced them that the less formal Low Mass was more appropriate, because that was the ceremony President Kennedy had preferred.

On the day of the funeral, the White House was jammed with heads of state who had flown in from all over the world on just a few hours' notice. According to Dad's former colleague Dr. Joe English,

It was the largest gathering of heads of state ever, and Angie Duke, the chief of protocol at the State Department, asked Sarge to greet them.

Sarge said yes, and then he asked me to grab a box of Mass cards. I got one just before they were taken to St. Matthew's Cathedral for the funeral Mass. I gave them to Sarge.

The first person he greeted was Haile Selassie, the emperor of Ethiopia, who was just over five feet tall. Selassie was crying when your dad handed him the card and said, "Your Majesty, I want this card to be a memorial of President Kennedy, who loved your country very much."

Selassie said to him, "President Kennedy needs no memorial in our country because he has three hundred of his children working there today," a reference to the Peace Corps volunteers.

Then your dad gave a card to French president Charles de Gaulle, who was six-five. The contrast between the two men—it was a surreal moment. Sarge went through

the entire room shaking hands and saying a word or two
to every leader, and every one of them was crying.

Throughout the ordeal, Dad was one of the few "Kennedy insiders" who maintained a working relationship with President Johnson and his advisers. During those tense days between the assassination and the funeral, Dad had to walk a tightrope between the grieving Kennedy family and the new president over issues of significant importance to the nation. When would Johnson make his first televised address to the country? When would he assume his place in the Oval Office? What Cabinet changes might he make?

Overhanging it all was the tension between President Johnson and Bobby. Indeed, Dad, while planning the funeral, met regularly with Johnson to urge him not to let paranoia and personal animosity interfere with appropriate mourning and a proper transition.

Dad's steadfastness, almost otherworldly, enabled him to command the attention of the grief-stricken, the power-hungry, and the anxiety-ridden alike.

As we were arranging for Dad's funeral, decades later, I heard about how masterfully he'd orchestrated my uncle's. I stayed up late the night after he died, plowing through files and scrapbooks, and I came across a photograph of the procession the day of Jack's funeral. Dad walked behind Jackie, as had been planned. Few cameras noticed him, but his gaze conveyed an assuredness and direction, a resolution, that almost no one else in the crowd had.

In an article written for *True* magazine months after the assassination, Robert Liston aptly captured Dad's central role in managing the myriad logistics behind Jack's funeral:

This scene, and those brutally emotional ones which pinned the world to its television sets for the next three days, came more out of Shriver than out of anyone else. Mrs. Kennedy's wishes were dominant, but it was he who translated them into the multiplicity of details which lent majesty to the national tragedy and moved a nation to tears.

He was, at times, the dynamic executive, forgetting personal feelings to get a tough job done well—and going without sleep and food in the process. He was the man of seemingly endless energy, still running strong when younger men were ready to drop. He was the aesthetic man of taste and sensitivity, the proper greeter of dignitaries at the White House and the family man in step behind Jacqueline Kennedy on her mournful march to her husband's funeral.

I am certain that Dad's central focus was not creating a majestic national funeral as much as it was instilling the faithfulness and the peacefulness of an eternal homecoming for the assassinated president. He was accompanying a president to be buried but, more important, he was hastening the soul of a loved one on the way to meet his Maker and know everlasting life.

That is a big supposition, but understanding the depth of Dad's faith now, I know that a proper funeral—a sacred ceremony—was foremost on his mind that day.

From addressing the rumored threat of another assassination to satisfying a nation's craving for solemn pageantry, from consoling a grieving widow to calming his grief-stricken, pregnant wife, from balancing a functioning government to honoring a dead man and his empty office, he fulfilled all his tasks with such grace because they were, simply, secondary. They were the things of this world—duties to be completed and completed well. But he wanted first and foremost to ensure a proper Catholic burial for the first Catholic president of the United States. Proper passage to life with God was what his dead brother-in-law most deserved.

He enacted his faith on that first night. He wanted a crucifix to be placed on the coffin, but the only options found that late on a Friday were inappropriately elaborate. Instead, he sent a car to retrieve the simple crucifix from above his bed so that it could be laid on the president's casket. He removed it on the morning of the funeral. A few months later, sent by President Johnson to meet the pope, he took the crucifix down from his wall again and carried it to Rome to be blessed. A few days later, he asked the head of the Greek Orthodox Church to bless it. That crucifix hung over his bed for years, until he encased it in a concrete cross that now stands over his parents' grave site in Westminster, Maryland.

We are all born into a web of relationships and circumstances, tragedies and opportunities. As I was coming into this world, my family lived through parades in Ireland one day and a funeral procession soon after. We never get to choose. My life in a famous and often star-crossed American clan would not be without its trials and disappointments, but I had as my father a man who not only was faith-filled and disciplined but who also insisted, in large part because of his faith, on the grace and joy in life. He possessed, and insisted on to me and his family and friends, a sustaining and empowering awareness of God's active grace in the world. When I was a young boy, that quality in him saved me from hopelessness; as I became an adult, it slowly shaped my vision for how to live, especially once I had to undertake the stern stuff of living without him.

◇

CHAPTER 2

GOING TO THE CHAPEL

Growing up, we regularly visited the Shriver homestead in Union Mills, Maryland, where the Shrivers settled in the 1700s. The homestead, now a museum, is in the rolling countryside, not far from the Pennsylvania line, on the road to Gettysburg. The extended Shriver family lived there along Big Pipe Creek, a fast stream that powered a busy gristmill. They soon built a tannery and canning operation in addition to their farming complex. Dad was born and raised in Westminster, Maryland, which was just seven miles from Union Mills, but he spent his summers at the homestead, and in his eyes, it was his true home.

On one trip—I must have been six years old or so—we ate tomato aspic canned by the B. F. Shriver Canning Company. I can taste it still, so tart and sharp it shocked me.

Dad loved to go home and walk around the property. He was six foot one, with thick, graying hair, an athletic build, and energy in every step. He wore his customary coat and tie, but more as a sign of respect than formality. His handshake and warm, friendly smile immediately put everyone at ease.

He bounded out of the car, excited to show us his childhood home. He pointed out little bits of history with such enjoyment and respect that it gave me the awe for history I still have today.

"Let's go," he'd exclaim. "Now, watch your head as you walk in the front door. The ceilings are so low—this house was built years and years ago, when people weren't as tall as they are today."

I marveled at the low ceilings and warped floors. You could set a marble on the floor and it would roll to the other end of the room. Dad pointed out the room where Washington Irving spent the night and where James Audubon stayed as well. He showed me the German barrel organ that dated from 1780, which was used to entertain visitors. He showed me the section of the house that served as the first post office for Union Mills and the balcony, a replica of the one at Monticello, where the Shrivers made political speeches. He told me about his great-great-great-grandfather David Shriver, who served in the Maryland legislature for thirty years and was a member of the Revolutionary War's Committee of Safety and Maryland's Constitutional Convention.

Another story he often told was about his own grandfather Thomas Herbert Shriver, who, at sixteen years of age, led Confederate General J. E. B. Stuart and his cavalrymen to the Battle of Gettysburg. His parents allowed him to do so only after General Stuart promised to write a recommendation for him to Virginia Military Institute. He went to VMI the next year and later joined about three hundred of his fellow VMI cadets in a battle at New Market, Virginia. He was shot and wounded, but the cadets soundly defeated the 34th Massachusetts Regiment of the Union Army. Dad was proud of his grandfather, not just because he led General Stuart to Gettysburg but also because of his bravery during the war.

After the war, Thomas Herbert Shriver joined an older brother, B. Franklin Shriver, in creating the B. F. Shriver

Canning Company. He also represented Carroll County for one term in both the Maryland House of Representatives and the Maryland State Senate and was a delegate to the Democratic National Conventions of 1908 and 1912.

"Do you know he tried to become a priest?" Dad told me. "He entered the seminary twice but became ill both times. He decided that this was a sign that he was not called to the priesthood! When he was in the seminary, he became great friends with a fellow seminarian named James Gibbons, who would become the second American cardinal, and my godfather."

The stories flowed from Dad as we wandered through the homestead. One told about a drunken soldier who, during the Battle of Gettysburg, stumbled onto the property and raised hell. When an officer tried to discipline him, the soldier shot him dead. The bullet went through the officer and lodged in the mill's wall. And there it still was when Dad was a boy.

Dad took me up the hill and across the road, two hundred yards or so, to a home that his side of the family had built in 1826. We walked in the front door and Dad's pace quickened. "Let's go this way," he said, heading toward a side parlor. "This is where General Stuart played the family's Steinway piano and sang, 'If you want to be a bully boy, join the cavalry' before he went to fight in the Battle of Gettysburg."

He started to sing. "Please don't do that," I said. "Your voice is terrible." He loved to sing—partly, I am sure, to embarrass us kids. "What's the matter with my voice? Your mother thinks it's fantastic." He sang a few more words before he blurted out, "About fifty years after Stuart sang that song, I was sleeping in the bedroom on the floor above!"

Dad's parents were second cousins. His mother's side of the family was Catholic and Confederate; his father's branch of the Shriver family was Union and Protestant. The ill feelings about the Civil War persisted. "My aunt wouldn't allow

anyone dressed in a blue suit into the house. And when I
went to Yale and played sports against Harvard, my mother—
the daughter of J. E. B. Stuart's scout!—told me I couldn't
spend the night in Boston because that was the capital of the
Yankees. Your mother loves to hear that one!"

Something unsettling happened on one trip that I regis-
tered but did not process until I had grown older. Dad loved
to go to Mass in the tiny chapel the family had built at the
back of the house—the same place where the legendary James
Cardinal Gibbons of Baltimore used to say Mass with Dad as
his altar boy.

I remember walking into the chapel and being shocked
by the gravity of the place. I had been in plenty of churches
during my boyhood but never one this simple, small, and
hushed. I looked out the window at the beautiful scene outside, the trees and the yard. Dad said a few words about Cardinal Gibbons being his godfather and how his cousin
William and he had been altar boys at a dying Gibbons's last
Mass.

And then he went silent. He crossed himself and started
to pray. I had seen him pray countless times before, but this
time was different—it was like a physical transformation had
occurred. His eyes grew tighter, he hunched when he knelt
down, and he didn't seem to notice me next to him.

After a few minutes, we continued on our tour. But I felt
as if he had been taken elsewhere and had not fully returned.
That day, we were accompanied by a woman who was a
volunteer at the museum. Dad regaled her with stories about
the Shriver family—about his older brother, Herbert, building the first radio in western Maryland, about how, as a
youth, he'd look out his window at all the horse-drawn car-
riages bringing corn to be milled at the homestead.

He told us about a near-fatal childhood disease. "I almost
died from an inexplicable illness," he said. "The doctors told

my parents my days were numbered. But all the Shrivers, Catholics and Protestants, prayed to Mother Elizabeth Ann Seton of Emmitsburg, and I lived. I might be one of the miracles that made her a saint!"

After the tour, we sat for a while on the front porch. Dad was still a pretty well-known public figure, and the volunteer was delighted to spend some more time with him. Dad kept talking, moving onto more recent history. His mother had taught him that the Catholic Church and the Shriver family were most important, followed closely by the Democratic Party. "We became great friends with Maryland governor Albert Ritchie," he told us. "He used to visit us when we lived in Westminster. I'll never forget getting in a Ford Model T and driving up to Albany with my mom and brother to hear Al Smith accept the Democratic nomination in 1928. Governor Ritchie had almost won the Democratic nomination in 1924—that was a big deal in Maryland. He and Al Smith were friends. We were so excited to drive all the way to Albany, especially because Smith was the first Catholic to be nominated for president. There weren't enough chairs in the statehouse, and I sat on Governor Ritchie's lap through the whole speech. I was just a little bit younger than you, Mark, but I think I crushed old Ritchie's leg!"

He went on: "You know what Ritchie's main ideas were, don't you? It was states' rights and local government. He also stressed religious freedom—your mother thinks that the idea of religious freedom was introduced in Massachusetts, but the political leaders of Maryland created a document called the Declaration of Rights that created religious freedom in Maryland. That was before the idea was in the Declaration of Independence and before anyone in Massachusetts had the idea!" He chuckled at that. "Everyone thinks that I am such a strong supporter of big federal government, but that wasn't the way I was raised. It was always states' rights and local government, but when the states aren't protecting all citizens and the citizens aren't given a fair opportunity in life, then that's when the federal government has to get involved."

When the volunteer asked him what he thought of President Ronald Reagan, Dad sat taller in his chair and leaned toward her. Reagan was trying to eliminate funding for the Peace Corps, Legal Services, and other initiatives Dad had worked so hard to establish. Dad was particularly upset that when he was governor of California, Reagan had tried to eliminate federal funding for the California Rural Legal Assistance program. As a lawyer, Dad saw legal representation as a basic right in a free democracy. Reagan saw it otherwise and was trying now, as president, to eliminate Legal Services altogether.

And then, in the middle of lamenting the impact of Reagan's cuts on America's poor, Dad again grew almost as somber as he had moments before in the family chapel. He took his eyes off the volunteer and looked out at the gristmill across Big Pipe Creek. And he told us, with a sadness in his voice and his eyes that I had never seen, that his father was ruined financially and emotionally during the Great Depression. In 1923, his father had moved the family from Westminster to Baltimore, where he went into banking, and then again, in 1929, to New York City to become a founding partner of a new investment bank. The timing could not have been worse.

The Depression forced the family to move from apartment to apartment, each smaller than the last. The investment bank closed, and shortly thereafter, his father went bankrupt. His family struggled to pay the rent, and even for groceries and bus money. His father, Dad said, was never the same after the Depression; he suffered a heart attack in the spring of 1938 and died in June 1942. His mother, I inferred,

kept the family on its feet—both financially and emotionally. Dad had to cobble together money from friends, odd
jobs, and scholarships to go to Canterbury, Yale, and Yale
Law School.

Years later, he talked about this time in his life in his
final letter to us: "I often think of my own father, whose generous and valiant heart was almost broken during the Depression of the thirties when financial failure almost destroyed
his own sense of personal worth. My father and mother gave
me an unforgettable lesson in how to survive financial ruin
with grace and courage and class."

I remembered that day in Maryland some thirty years
later, when I visited my father at an assisted living facility in
Potomac that served as his final home.

I was sitting on his couch, holding his hand.

He blew his nose into his hands, as he had done thousands
of times over the last five years. I let out a groan and handed
him a tissue. He wiped his hand clean, or at least as clean as it
was going to get, and threw the tissue on the floor. I got up and
put it in the trash can. He said, "Thank you." It was always the
same routine.

I sat back down and grabbed his hand again, and that's
when I remembered that beautiful day in western Maryland.
And I realized that my father had seen worse.

Little did I know that loving him through those final years
would constitute the first true test of my spiritual mettle—
a test that, even though it came so much later in my life than
did his, I was less prepared to meet.

◇

CHAPTER 3

SOLDIER OF FAITH

So I knew that he had endured darkness and struggle. But it was what he experienced during World War II that must have most strongly tested and, ultimately, confirmed his faith. He took seriously the Christian virtue of humility, and when it came time for a war story he beamed and looked knowingly at his questioner but rarely said much.

One night, a few years after graduating from the College of the Holy Cross, my roommates and I gathered for cocktails with Dad. This had become a ritual for us—when we were together in Washington, we would head over to my parents'.

"What would you like to drink—a vodka tonic, some wine, or are you boys still drinking beers?" he'd ask. "My God, I thought you drank every last beer there was during college." And then he'd make another offer, opening a small humidor: "Anybody want a stogie? I can't figure out how to work this damn thing, but what the hell, these are pretty good cigars." He would pass them out and look with great admiration at his own cigar, lick it side to side, and clip the end with a cigar cutter. "That's what you're supposed to do. Let's light 'em up!"

My friends' questions usually had to do with politics or

the Kennedys or the Peace Corps. Dad loved to tell them stories, especially about trekking through the jungles of the Philippines or the African bush or—his favorite—hunting with French president Charles de Gaulle.

With a drink in one hand, a cigar in the other, and a smile on his face, he'd clear his throat and say, "Have I told you the one about de Gaulle?"

Of course we'd heard it countless times, but every rendition had a different flair. "I have heard it once or twice, Dad," I'd say, "but these guys haven't. Tell it to them."

"Great! Come on over here." He'd puff on his cigar one more time. "Now, you know de Gaulle was six foot five." He'd stand ramrod straight and jut out his chest. Everyone would laugh.

"I was the newly installed ambassador to France, and our two countries weren't getting along too well. Vietnam was happening, and there was a geopolitical power struggle. But de Gaulle and I hit it off immediately. One day, he invited me to the countryside for a pheasant shoot with a number of other ambassadors. We stood around waiting for about thirty minutes before de Gaulle arrived in a long black car and emerged fully dressed in military gear. He was so tall and big—what a physically towering figure he was! Now, the American ambassador was one of the most important ambassadorships, so I found myself standing closest to de Gaulle, about fifteen feet from him."

A whistle was blown and Dad heard the "beaters," the guys who flushed the birds out of the woods and into the open field to be shot by the ambassadors, all of whom were lined up. As the birds flew, one bird avoided all of the shots. Dad would weave and bob himself as he told us of the bird's flight. And then Dad had the last shot.

At this point he would smile and say, "You guessed right— *bam!* And damn if that bird didn't head straight for de Gaulle.

I looked at de Gaulle, I looked at the bird, I looked back at de Gaulle and he was not flinching at all. The dead bird landed *smack* at his feet!

"And I said to de Gaulle, '*Un cadeau pour vous, Monsieur le Président!*' (A gift for you, Mr. President.)

."And de Gaulle replied, '*Bon coup, Monsieur l'Ambassadeur.*' (Good shot, Mr. Ambassador.)

"And I replied, '*Merci infiniment, Monsieur le Président!*'" (Thank you very much, Mr. President!)

We'd all roar with laughter, and Dad would, too.

But this time the conversation turned to the war. I knew that the day after Dad took his final exam at Yale Law School, he joined the navy, missing his law school graduation, and I knew that he later served on the USS *South Dakota* and on a submarine. I loved to hear him describe living on a sub and moving around the torpedoes. "There were four tubes forward, six tubes aft," he would explain, "and the quarters were incredibly cramped. We weren't allowed to discuss religion, politics, or women because those topics always ended up in fistfights."

One of my buddies asked Dad where he was when Pearl Harbor was bombed, and we got the same blow-by-blow account I had heard many times, both in person and in a few of the many letters he wrote me over the years: He was in command of the Third Naval District in New York and heard the bulletin about the bombing of Pearl Harbor while listening to a radio broadcast of a Giants football game at the Polo Grounds. He immediately telephoned his brother, Herbert, who was on duty at the Brooklyn Navy Yard, to be sure that he heard the news—and to assure himself it wasn't a hoax. And then he mobilized the entire division, irritating many absent officers, who were stunned by the decisiveness of a junior officer manning the weekend shift.

He went on to tell us that, once the country entered the

war, he wasn't even allowed to leave the USS *South Dakota* when it was in port in Annapolis, Maryland, to attend his father's funeral in nearby Baltimore. I still cannot fathom that: he was twenty miles away and could not attend the funeral—I would have been crushed.

My buddies probed for more, and Dad came up with another story, this one a bit more explicit but still acceptable to his sensibilities. He wrote about it in a letter to me on December 7, 2000:

> I thought you might be interested to receive . . . the attached postal card. In case you didn't recognize it immediately, it is a painting . . . of the USS Dakota in that ship's battle with the Japanese at the rather famous location of Santa Cruz.
>
> It was a famous battle because it was primarily a battle between Japanese Air Force and USA surface ships. As you can see, the anti-aircraft guns of the South Dakota were firing away at the Japanese airplanes, some of which are depicted as crashing in flames.
>
> I was in command of all the anti-aircraft guns on the starboard side of the South Dakota all the way from the bow back to the middle of the ship. . . . I don't think we lost any sailors. . . . Everyone on the South Dakota . . . rejoiced in the decisive victory. . . . I am happy to say I was lucky enough to get by with simply one piece of shrapnel which hit my upper left arm and caused some loss of blood, but nothing else.

But this time he kept going with a story I had never heard—about an attack on his ship during the Battle of Guadalcanal. He told us how he slipped on the blood of his buddies as it flowed down the ship's stairs; how, after beating back the Japanese, he had to clean up his friends' body parts from the ship's deck. He told us how the ship and crew endured hellish combat and how he prayed to God throughout the night that he would live to see the next day. He was so exhausted that after the battle was over, he collapsed on his bed and fell asleep still wearing his bloody clothes.

He woke up and never looked back. He picked belief in spite of every reason not to believe. That, I suppose, is what faith is. The leap of belief in spite of no evidence.

The faithful often come to their belief through the proverbial dark night of the soul. That night, on a stinking, battle-scarred ship bouncing on rough waters, he no doubt had his moment.

When sons like me—sons of the greatest generation— realize the gravity of our fathers' obligations, we are struck by how much more daunting they were than any obstacles we have faced. For me, that created a sense not of shame or inadequacy but simply of awe.

His name itself had a military resonance. He loved to tell the story of how, when he was on a navy ship during the war, his mother somehow managed to reach his vessel to ask that he be paged. The officer on duty told her, "There ain't no sergeants in the navy, ma'am!" When she kept insisting that there was, he hung up on her.

Now, looking back, I can't help wondering at the coincidence of it all—how a guy named Sargent was not just a brave fighter in a great war but also a Christian soldier, not because of his name but, in large part, because of how he lived. He was a disciplined believer, practicing faith with a military resoluteness. I saw it every day I was with him, though I couldn't articulate it this concisely and—at least for me—usefully until after he died. Still, half a grasp was better than no grasp at all, and Dad's faithfulness helped make my boyhood enchanting and the darker days of my adolescence bearable.

CHAPTER 4

◇

GROWING UP A SON OF SARGE

On March 22, 1976, my father dropped out of the race for the Democratic nomination for the presidency. I was twelve years old, adored him, and was enchanted by the magical carpet ride that a campaign could be for a boy. But every child experiences, sooner or later, the astounding realization that their parent is shaken. You aren't privy to the cause or the details, but you sense it in the adult's demeanor. You sense it with an almost animal-like instinct and alarm. I felt that sensation for the first time that morning.

We went to the National Press Club in Washington, where a decent-sized crowd had assembled to hear his withdrawal speech. He smiled throughout it, but its content, I realized long after, was startling. I obviously didn't understand at the time how what he said then would inform my quest during the days after his death:

> What we need now is not the false security of beguiling promises or befogging rhetoric, not empty and simplistic slogans. We need the spiritual confidence borne of confronting openly and honestly the challenges—the terrors in the nights—we all know, we all must face. One of those challenges is the continuing need to empower the powerless.

When he finished, everyone gathered around to hug him and shake his hand, and so many people were crying that it scared me. Everyone was acting like Dad wasn't just leaving the race but was taking leave of the planet. We exited the Press Club, jumped into the car the Secret Service had waiting out front, and headed to National Airport for a family escape in the Dominican Republic.

I loved having the Secret Service around—each agent looked like he was straight out of the movies or on a pro football team, and nothing was more fun for a boy than to throw a football or a baseball with athletic guys who were willing to give their lives to ensure his dad's safety. They were heroes to me.

But my idealized image crumbled when the lead agent walked us to the door of the plane that day and said, "Mr. Shriver, can you sign this document please?"

Dad turned around and took the piece of paper. They exchanged a few words, and Dad signed it and handed it back. When they shook hands, I noticed them looking each other in the eye just a little bit longer than usual. Then the man turned around and strode back up the walkway. Dad boarded the airplane, and I followed him. The door closed behind us. The Secret Service was gone; my heroes were gone.

We didn't talk much on the flight to the Dominican Republic, and when we landed we gathered our own bags and hailed a cab to the hotel. There was no Secret Service to meet us; there wasn't even a car waiting. I will never forget that sense of loss—I felt abandoned by the greatest group of playmates a kid could ever ask for. It was like a punch in the gut. What had just happened? I learned at that moment that fame, fortune, and adulation are gone the minute you're out of politics. I never forgot that when I went into politics myself. As soon as you're out, you're out.

And yet the only two times I saw my dad shaken were during his speech to his team at the hotel and when he said good-bye to that Secret Service agent. Piecing it all back together, I can say now that he was uniquely unmoved by it all, except when he had to bid farewell to people he felt he had let down.

Dad had something very few people, let alone politicians, can summon: constancy. As I look back at his life and our relationship, I believe the source of this constancy was his radical faith. He was ambitious, but it was more a cosmic ambition than an egotistical one. His concession speech surprises me to this day: his talk of "spiritual confidence" and "terrors in the night" stray intentionally into the land of faith—a place where Democratic politicians are not supposed to go. And yet he was a Democrat, a liberal, a public servant, precisely because of his faith. Politics was the best professional venue for him to act out his faith; there he could exercise that cosmic ambition for justice and equality.

Yes, Dad had an ego—you have to have a strong ego to stand up and run for political office at any level in this country, let alone vice president or president. But so many politicians say that they go into politics because of a desire to serve, and though that may be true initially, for many of them, the longer they stay, the more it becomes about being called "the honorable" this or that, the more it becomes about people being deferential to their opinions, about people kissing their fannies, about being on television, about dinners with rich people or movie stars at the best tables. The office becomes conflated with the power and the prestige. Most politicians cling to that, desperately.

President Clinton said it well when he spoke at Dad's funeral: "There is nothing closer to death than being defeated in politics; being defeated and doing it in a way that gives you public humiliation is agonizing."

A typical politician will avoid that public humiliation at all costs. But Dad's deep faith rooted his ego in a desire to do God's will. I honestly believe that he saw the creation of the Peace Corps and the creation of the War on Poverty as a calling to do God's will at that moment in time. The same could be said of his work on the Chicago Board of Education or the Catholic Interracial Council or the '72 ticket or the '76 run. He did the best he could, and then he moved on. He was a fundamentalist—but not in the sense that he imposed his religious views on anyone. He just lived his faith; it was the driver of his work.

President Clinton understood this. He said,

Thirty years later [after the '72 race], I saw the next thing that is most painful for people in politics, and that is where you're done and nobody cares whether you are winning or losing. Better to be humiliated than ignored, right? So, I wonder—I swear, I couldn't make this up. I'm in Miami and Anthony has got his dad down there, and we're all gonna go to dinner with two, maybe three of the people who were there that night, who are in this church. And we go to this kinda tony restaurant, which as I remember was in the South Beach area, and I show up—I thought I looked pretty cool; I've got a blue shirt on and a blue sports coat, you know. Sargent Shriver shows up, eighty-seven years old, in a double-breasted blue sports coat, seersucker pants, and these unbelievable shoes with Romero Britto art on them. As God is my witness, I'm sitting there and all these really cool dudes are walking by, you know it's Miami, and they're looking at his feet: *Hmm . . . who is this guy?* He kept us laughing all night long; he had more energy than anybody else. What difference did it make if he wasn't powerful anymore; he had today, a gift of God.

President Clinton had it right, almost.

Dad really wasn't a politician, at least not a modern-day version of an American politician, Republican or Democrat. I don't think he ever looked at his defeats and thought, *I am not powerful anymore*. It didn't take him thirty years or, really, any time to get over the losses, because that type of thinking never entered his mind. The guy who kept Clinton laughing all night long, who had more energy than anyone else at eighty-seven, was the same guy in the Dominican Republic thirty years earlier, hailing a cab and talking about the beauty of the transparent blue water hours after walking away from the race for the biggest job in the world. He was the same guy who called me the day after I lost my congressional race in 2002 and acted as if nothing had changed. In fact, he wasn't acting. In his book, nothing had changed. His faith saw to that. The sort of election loss, or two, that would be interpreted by most politicians as an agonizing blow to their very being was, for Dad, a blip on his cosmic screen.

I don't really understand the psychology of religion or the origins of faith. But I do believe that his suffering and trials made his faith stronger. That much I get. He was born into the faith of his family, but his experience made his faith personal, stronger, and animating. Good God, to believe like he did!

I am certain a day never passed when he did not recall the blood of his shipmates and the loss of their lives; I have tried to imagine the strength it took for him to orchestrate one of the most tragic funerals in American history; I can't imagine surviving the Great Depression with a father who was bankrupted and despondent and then not being able to go to his funeral.

In his final letter to us, Dad wrote, about his parents, "Their experience helped convince me that putting trust in money or in any economic system is absurd. It is wiser and safer to trust in our Lord than in banks or gold or the New York Stock Exchange."

It was his faith in a different system that kept his eyes on a richer wealth, a bigger prize. Going to Mass daily, having a daily relationship with God, even a minute-by-minute relationship with God—that's what gave Dad "power," gave him his hope. That hope, enabled by that faith, was there in good times and in bad, in D.C. in '63 and in '72 and in '76 and in Miami Beach when he was eighty-seven.

He was always animated by hope, yet I wouldn't need to fully grasp the depth of his hope until after he had taken his last breath. For most of my life, it was enough for me to feed off his energy—he carried all of us on his wave. He kept us believing; he kept us hopeful. When he walked into a room, you just felt better. You felt ready for the day.

HOPE

We were once a symbol of hope not because we manipulated events abroad but because we embraced ideals that moved nations and shook the world. We can be a symbol of hope again.

—S<small>ARGENT</small> S<small>HRIVER</small>, Announcement for
President, Mayflower Hotel,
Washington, D.C.
September 20, 1975

CHAPTER 5

KEEPING UP WITH
THE KENNEDYS

My brother Bobby was playing football on the lawn in Hyannis Port one summer day in the mid-1960s when he ran into one of our cousins, fell down, and slowly but surely started to cry.

Uncle Bobby was standing nearby and said, "Kennedys don't cry!"

Dad heard him but didn't look his way. Instead, he walked straight toward my brother and lifted him up.

"It's okay, you can cry! You're a Shriver!"

With that exultant permission, Bobby actually began to cry less. Dad's cheerful blessing of a supposedly shameful act seemed to distract Bobby from his boo-boo.

I have heard this story so many times that I feel I was actually there. I may have been, but I would have been about four years old. The story, nonetheless, is a part of me. The incident was one of the few moments of visible dissonance between Dad and his more famous brothers-in-law and father-in-law. He was a team player, their loyal political partner and family member, but he could separate his identity from the clan's internal pressure to achieve greatness. I could not.

Growing up in a big, competitive, public family with

countless cousins, I never allowed myself to calm down. There was relentless competition on the athletic field and in the classroom. I had a very strong sense that we kids were competing against a past that always won.

My boyhood home, Timberlawn, in Rockville, Maryland, was a bustling central station where sports and chaos and love all competed for time and attention. My parents rented the place, a two-hundred-acre functioning farm where cows and horses dotted the rolling hills, pigs, chickens, and sheep made their noises all around us, and Bobby even had a pet monkey. The pond was filled with snapping turtles, fish, and frogs, and we had a canoe for adventures. We used to dodge all the animals and the family dogs in our go-kart.

There were endless visitors, such as President Johnson, Olympic gold medalist Rafer Johnson, and Washington Redskins quarterback Sonny Jurgensen; Davis Cup captain Donald Dell (also my godfather) was always around, often accompanied by Arthur Ashe or Stan Smith; the columnist Art Buchwald was one of my parents' best friends, as was the legendary trial lawyer and Baltimore Orioles owner Edward Bennett Williams, and they were regular guests. There were events with people like César Chávez, Archbishop William Baum of Washington, D.C., Neil Diamond, and Barbra Streisand. Cloris Leachman and Carol Channing stopped by, as did Father Ted Hesburgh, the president of Notre Dame, and Dad's law school classmate Byron (Whizzer) White, the onetime NFL star who'd been appointed to the Supreme Court by President Kennedy. Former Peace Corps staffers such as Bill Moyers and Harris Wofford didn't even need to knock.

There was nonstop action inside the house, too. Mom and Dad hired Goldie, a woman with developmental disabilities, to do the laundry, clean the house, and help serve dinner. She had thick glasses and smoked like a chimney and was not averse to cursing or telling you exactly how she was feeling. One time when a number of cousins were over for dinner and too many people were asking Goldie for seconds, she grabbed a piece of chicken from the serving dish she was holding and threw it onto someone's plate. "Here's your goddamn chicken," she yelled. "Don't ask me for any more." Then she turned, serving dish in hand, and stormed into the kitchen. No one asked for more food.

But most of all, athletic competition defined us. I was a big kid and a good athlete. I loved football and particularly loved to play with my brothers and, boy, did I love to beat whoever I lined up against! If you lost, you knew you were going to hear about it at dinner and it was going to be hard to take.

We ran countless drills in the backyard. Timmy was the quarterback, and Anthony and I would rotate offense and defense. When friends came over, we'd pick sides and go at it.

I loved the competition, especially with Timmy's older friends. They were bigger and better than Anthony and I, which made it even sweeter when we scored against them.

Our games would go on for hours. Eventually there would be blood and bruises. Dad played alongside us, and he did not shy away from the pushing and shoving and elbowing on the line of scrimmage. In his early to mid-sixties, Dad was competing against high school juniors and seniors. After football games, we would head to the pool for water polo. The kids would be divided up, and the whole scene would happen all over again. The variation we played did not resemble water polo as played anywhere else on earth. If someone had the ball, you were allowed to dunk them and hold them under the water until they let go of the ball or wiggled away from you. Dunking was not only allowed, it was encouraged.

If you had the ball and wanted to score, you had to hold the ball on the opponent's wall for a count of "three Mississippi." Of course, if someone could knock the ball off the wall by two and a half, the goal didn't count.

No one ever drowned or even lost a tooth, as far as I can remember, but there were bloody lips and scrapes and plenty of shouting matches. I can still conjure the image of Mom dunking Anthony and holding him down in the deep end of the pool until he let go of the ball and emerged, gasping for air.

After water polo, Dad would hit us fly balls, or we might just beg off and ride the go-kart around the place. Of course, it was illegal to have a brother or a friend ride on the wheel cover, but that didn't stop us. That go-kart could hit thirty-five miles an hour, and with at least two dogs running alongside, trying to bite the tires and occasionally getting your leg, the action didn't diminish until you were called for dinner.

Dinner was either a triumph or a disaster, depending on how you'd done athletically. Every play was relived, every goal recounted, every dropped fly ball retold.

When the topic of books came up at supper, you were regularly reminded to read the series on great Americans, including the volume entitled *Meet John F. Kennedy*. I didn't memorize any of Uncle Jack's speeches, but his inaugural address, signed and framed, hung in two locations, alongside speeches by Uncle Bobby and Uncle Teddy, and there were busts of both Jack and Bobby in the house. I don't remember when I learned the "Ask not" quote or the *"Ich bin ein Berliner"* line—they were just always there in my memory.

And so, too, was the answer to that oft-repeated trivia question: "Who was the youngest elected president?" If you answered Theodore Roosevelt, you were wrong. Teddy

Roosevelt became the youngest president at forty-two, when he succeeded the assassinated William McKinley; he wasn't elected in his own right until he was forty-six. Jack won on his own at the age of forty-three.

And when Grandma Kennedy visited, she always had a few questions to test your grammar skills. Her favorite was "Is it correct to say 'if I were president' or 'if I was president'?"

If you answered "was," she'd laugh and say, "No, dear, it is 'if I were president.' You use 'were' because it is contrary to fact. You aren't president, at least not yet."

During summers in Hyannis Port, the athletic competition increased as all the cousins gathered. One had only to look at the walls inside the Hyannis Port Yacht Club to see the name Kennedy everywhere for races won. If you didn't win the junior races, Mom would remind you that her dad always made her brothers and her go out and practice after their losses.

Sailboat racing with older cousins was exhilarating and nerve-racking. It was an honor to be asked to crew on the sailboat, but the races were tense affairs. If you made a mistake, you could count on getting yelled at and, oftentimes, punched.

The football games in Grandma Kennedy's backyard went on for hours, and it was not unusual to have plenty of yelling and screaming over calls. People did whatever it took to win, including diving into the rosebushes that lined parts of the field in an effort to catch a pass. Michael Kennedy, who was a fantastic football player, frequently emerged from the rosebushes with the ball in hand, smiling and bleeding from the thorns.

Hyannis Port was a seemingly ideal place to spend childhood summers. There were motorboats and sailboats, tennis and golf (but we didn't play golf—it was too slow), softball and football games, bikes, and, of course, tourists. Lots of tourists looking for the Kennedy compound and hoping to see a real live Kennedy, no matter the age.

When we kids rode our bikes around that small town, tourists often asked for directions, then did a double take. Perhaps the thick, long hair and the big teeth gave us away; whatever it was, the second question was inevitably "Are you a Kennedy?"

If you told the truth, there would be squeals of delight, and the entire family would scramble out of the car and ask for a quick picture or two.

I have no idea what people did with those pictures, but it felt good to make them smile. Soon some cousin discovered that it was even nicer if they smiled as they were buying a "Kennedy candle." Amazingly enough, there was a small candle company about three-quarters of a mile from the compound, and the owner, Marvin Blank, was a good friend of Mom's. Mom had convinced Mr. Blank to hire people with developmental disabilities and to create and sell a Rose Kennedy candle. The money from those candles went to Special Olympics.

I am pretty sure that Mr. Blank knew that my cousins and I jumped into his dumpster and took his discarded wax in the evenings. His son Brad was one of our best friends and a regular accomplice in these adventures. We put the wax into a big pot, melted it, then poured it into a hole in the sand, stuck a string in it, and let it sit. Voilà! A Kennedy candle, and with Kennedy sand to boot! We set up tables outside the compound and sold them to tourists for cash.

You have to remember that this was the 1970s: Uncle Bobby had died just a few years earlier, Dad had been ambassador to France and was the Democratic vice presidential candidate in 1972, Uncle Teddy was rumored to run every cycle, and in 1976, Dad did run for president. By the end of the decade, Teddy was running for president against Jimmy Carter. The Kennedys were always on the national news. We also had our own internal news channel—the one that spread updates on a cousin's achievements, particularly in sports, to all the other cousins like wildfire—and I was consumed by it. When I was ten, it looked like I would end up well over six feet tall, but that growth spurt never happened. I grew outward instead of upward, and the suddenly chunky Shriver attracted nicknames like glue: Fatty, the Blob, Tubby, and so on.

The pressure mounted: the painful nicknames, the athletic contests, the competition to sell Kennedy candles (even though we were Shrivers), the political tension. The result was that I struggled, especially during the fourth, fifth, and sixth grades at St. Albans. If you can picture an old-line, strict, Episcopalian, English-style prep school catering to the upper class of Washington, you've got St. Albans. There weren't grades; there were "forms." Form A was fourth grade, Form B fifth, Form C sixth. The principal was called the headmaster, and it seemed as if every kid had a famous and powerful father who was a senator or ambassador. If you graduated at the bottom of your class, you were still headed to an Ivy League school because the academics were that good and you were that well connected.

I didn't last long. After three years at St. Albans, at the age of twelve, I transferred to my third school, Potomac, where I would stay for seventh, eighth, and ninth grades. The move meant a little less academic stress, but it also meant coed classes for the first time, as well as having cousins as classmates and schoolmates. Chris Kennedy had been at Potomac for six years and had a ton of friends; we were now in the same class, a year ahead of his brother Max, two years ahead of my brother Anthony, and four and five years ahead of Douglas and Rory Kennedy.

Adolescence is a formative and tumultuous time, and I struggled mightily. A large, chaotic, highly competitive family is a fun but demanding environment in which to grow up; the public eye made it that much more difficult. The St. Albans years were particularly hard. The academic stress at St. Albans, where I at least made what they called the effort honor roll consistently, though never the academic honor roll until my final marking period; the teasing about my weight; the competition in the classroom and in sports; plus the absurd strain of growing up in the Kennedy family—all of this combined to make me a bear to live with. I was angry, and I took it out on my family and friends. I screamed a lot at everybody in the house.

As I reflect on the timing of this difficult period, I can see now the turmoil in our lives, but I don't remember Dad speaking to me about why I was so angry. I don't remember a conversation about the academic pressure of St. Albans, the nicknames, the chaos, or the athletic competition in the family.

I think that Dad's generation simply didn't have those conversations with their kids. Clearly, he had a lot on his mind, but I honestly believe that even if he hadn't run for vice president and president, he still wouldn't have had that sort of conversation with me.

The result was that I wanted desperately to be known as Mark Shriver, but how could I do that when I was surrounded by the myths of yesterday, the hopes of tomorrow, and countless cousins who looked a lot like me? I was angry; I was struggling to hope. I was aware of the virtue of hopefulness. Dad exuded it; I was lunging for it. I knew he was different—good God, he thought it was okay to cry in a family that didn't tolerate such displays! But he never pulled me aside to give me a "hope" lecture akin to the talk he gave me, once I began dating, about treating young women with respect. Yet his work and his demeanor kept me hoping that I would find a more peaceful place to be able to make sense of what I had been born into.

◇

CHAPTER 6

PEACE WORK

Growing up, I saw the Peace Corps and Special Olym-pics as extended family. These organizations were so much a part of the daily fabric of our lives that as a child I never really thought about their origins. Mom was the founder and public face of Special Olympics, just as Dad was of the Peace Corps. But they were both as involved with each oth-er's "babies" as their own. They sought each other's advice, helped each other plan the growth of both institutions, and, more than anything, enjoyed sharing in each other's worlds. Mom was always happy when she was at a Peace Corps celebration; likewise, I never saw Dad more joyous than when he attended a Special Olympics event. They rel-ished each other's work.

I loved meeting Peace Corps volunteers and hearing their stories. Dad's high energy level would increase even more whenever he met a Peace Corps volunteer. He'd pep-per them with questions: What country did you serve in? What did you do? What did you like? What didn't you like?

One time I watched as he mesmerized a group gathered on the back porch. He told us that he had landed in some Asian country after sleeping on the floor of the airplane, below the seats, which was his habit. He didn't have time to go to the hotel to shower, so he freshened up in the airport bathroom.

Dad entered the president's office, they shook hands and sat down, and no one spoke. Dad waited. And waited. The president just sat there without speaking, without blinking, without even moving.

"In a Westernized country, we would have exchanged pleasantries, chatted about our children—we would have said something!" Dad exclaimed. "I was wondering what the hell was going on, but I waited for him to speak first."

After ten minutes, when the president did finally open his mouth, it was to tell Dad that the Peace Corps was welcome. The organization would know how to respect local custom if its founder and leader could.

From stories like these, at an early age I had a sense of the world, of geography, because places like the Philippines and Chile and Haiti were regularly discussed at dinner. To me, that was just part of my dad's job, and I had little sense of the uniqueness of his work.

In fact, I first heard the story of the founding of the Peace Corps from Mom. Dad was traveling in the Soviet Union and Mom decided to hold a course for me on what Dad had done years before. She wasn't much for reflecting on past events—she was always so consumed with the tasks of the day that she rarely looked back—but this time was different.

She began with her brother's first public mention of the concept.

On October 13, 1960, Jack had flown straight from New York and his third debate with Nixon to address students at the University of Michigan. He arrived at two A.M. on the morning of the fourteenth after a flight delay. Thousands of enthusiastic students had waited into the wee hours, hoping their candidate would show up. In response to the students' energy, Jack made extemporaneous remarks:

"How many of you," he shouted, "who are going to be doctors are willing to spend your days in Ghana?" As the crowd roared its affirmation, Jack continued: "On your willingness to do that, not merely to serve one year or two years in the service, but on your willingness to contribute part of your life to this country, I think will depend the answer [to] whether a free society can compete."

Less than a month later, Jack won the presidency. The next day, he asked Dad to lead the hiring effort for Cabinet-level jobs; Dad was the headhunter for assembling the legendary "best and brightest." Scott Stossel, in his biography of my father, *Sarge*, enumerated several reasons why Uncle Jack gave this crucial assignment to Dad: Dad had demonstrated excellent judgment throughout the campaign; he had an eye for talent, as evidenced by those whom he had brought on board for the race; and he had what was thought to be the widest range of acquaintances, from Catholic bishops and African American publishing executives to Supreme Court justices.

"Though people were sometimes ruffled by Shriver's courtesy and easy amiability into dismissing him as something of a Boy Scout," Arthur Schlesinger wrote in his 1965 book *A Thousand Days*, "the President-elect had confidence in his energy and imagination—a confidence Shriver had justified in the campaign and justified again now."

And it was that imagination that recruited Republicans like Douglas Dillon to be secretary of the Treasury and Bob McNamara (the newly named leader of Ford Motor Company) to be secretary of Defense. The Harvard economics professor David Bell was recruited to run the Bureau of the Budget (now called the Office of Management and Budget). Dad identified Dean Rusk as secretary of state and staffed his office with Adlai Stevenson as U.N. ambassador, Chester Bowles as undersecretary of state, and Michigan governor G. Mennen Williams as undersecretary of state for Africa.

But all the while the president labored to find the best position in the administration to realize Dad's talents.

Dad rejected several proposals—jobs at State, Justice, even high-level White House staff positions. He held out for a position with the real power to effect change; otherwise he wanted to return to his adopted home of Chicago and potentially run for governor of Illinois, as many people there were encouraging him to do.

The Peace Corps idea, meanwhile, seemed destined for the waste bin of so many political campaign promises. That is, until the president offered the job to Dad. The day after he was sworn in, Jack called Dad at his Chicago home and asked him to create the Peace Corps.

Dad struggled with the offer because the opportunity in Illinois pulled strongly at him. But in the end, he couldn't resist taking command of a compelling idea that, if fulfilled, would help spread hope around the world. I use the word "idea" because that was all Dad really took charge of—a vision that no one had fleshed out beyond a few campaign conversations. Not only was there no funding for the project, but existing foreign aid agencies posed significant opposition.

The odds of making the idea a reality were stacked against Dad. Former president Eisenhower mockingly dubbed the Peace Corps a "juvenile experiment," and in an editorial entitled "It's a Puzzlement," the *Wall Street Journal* wrote,

> The thing is so completely disproportionate as to be non-sensical. The wars of the civilized world did not break out because there was any lack of peoples-to-peoples contact between Germans and Frenchmen. . . . What person—except perhaps the very young themselves—can really believe that an Africa aflame with violence will

have its fires quenched because some Harvard boy or Vassar girl lives in a mud hut and speaks Swahili?

Foreign governments accused the effort of being a vehicle for American infiltration (read: spying) of their cultures. Dad even joked publicly that he was given the job because Jack had told him that if it failed, it would be easier "to fire a relative than a political friend."

Yet Dad, through grueling months of strategic lobbying, cajoling, hell-raising, and insisting, almost single-handedly turned a wobbly idea into an enduring entity. He appeared on *Meet the Press* to persuade the nation; he constantly went to the Hill to lobby; and he traveled the country encouraging and being encouraged by all the young people who wanted him to deliver on the president's promise.

When Mom told me about all this, I was struck by the pride she took in the story. She was as persistent a person as I have ever or will ever meet. And when she got to the part of the story in which she recounted how Dad just wouldn't quit, I sensed why they were so attracted to each other. They were soul mates because they were workmates. They woke up each morning with determination on their faces. They walked out to meet the world as comrades in their common causes.

The Peace Corps, for Dad, was an antidote to all the espionage and intrigue and mistrust of the geopolitical era. I found out after Dad died that in the entrance to the original Peace Corps building, he had hung a sign with ten words:

"If they mean to have peace, let it begin here."

Now, these words speak for themselves. But Dad's sign was also a reference to a famous quotation that would certainly resonate with Revolutionary War history buffs and schoolchildren in Massachusetts. For there is a monument on Lexington Common in Lexington, Massachusetts, dedicated to the first battle of the Revolutionary War—a monument that also memorializes the words Captain John Parker spoke to the Minutemen he commanded that day, just before the first shots in the first battle were fired: "If they mean to have a war, let it begin here."

In Dad's mind, the Peace Corps was the beginning of a revolution—a revolution for peace. "If they mean to have peace, let it begin here."

But what kind of revolution did Dad think he was starting?

"The Peace Corps is different," he told the Foreign Policy Association in December 1963. "It goes beyond politics and national rivalries to reach the deepest hopes of man. It is a working model, a microcosm, a small society representing the kind of world we want our children to live in."

But what is the driving force of this revolution? What takes us beyond violence, beyond politics and national rivalries, to realize our deepest hopes for the kind of world we want our children to live in? In a speech at Fordham University, Dad stated the foundational principle of his revolution: "Compassion and service," he said, "shatter barriers of politics and creed; [they] dissolve obstacles of race and belief anywhere in the world."

Dad built these revolutionary ideals into the Peace Corps and they guided the work of the volunteers in the field. As he explained to the Foreign Policy Association:

> Our volunteers [do not] go overseas as the salesmen of a particular political theory, or economic system, or religious creed. They go to work *with* people, not to employ them, use them or advise them. They do what the country they go to *wants them to do*, not what we think is best. They live among the people, sharing their homes, eating

their food, talking their language, living under their laws, not in special compounds with special privileges.

"Compassion is the ideal," he maintained in a speech at the World's Fair in 1964, "that must illuminate, from the very center, all our efforts to bring a better life to our world, within our own country, and in the farthest reaches of the planet." As he went on to say: "It is only with this compassion that man can look upon man—through the mask of many colors, through the vestments of many religions, through the dust of poverty, or through the disfigurement of disease—and recognize his brother."

But Dad knew that this was not easy. Even for himself.

After Dad died, I came across a speech he gave on February 7, 1968, at the University of Notre Dame Student Assembly. It startled me. It told a story I had never heard before.

I'll never forget, in Malaysia, going through a local hospital where we had two or three Peace Corps nurses. One of them worked in the leper ward and said to me, 'Mr. Shriver, you've got to come see my ward.' I didn't want to see her ward, but how could I say no if that girl was in there? So I went, and I'll never forget when I grabbed that first [hand] and shook it. I was scared. I shouldn't have been, but I was. That girl worked there to bring peace on earth. Not the abstract kind of peace that politicians talk about, but the peace that men feel in their bones when they are loved, or fed, or clothed, or housed.

It stunned me that Dad talked about hope and compassion and service, about shattering barriers, but he, the leader of that effort, hesitated when presented with just such an opportunity. Dad didn't want to go into a leper ward where Peace Corps volunteers worked? He was scared of shaking hands with someone with leprosy? He was following the lead of a young Peace Corps nurse and not leading?

He hadn't been totally fearless and unwavering after all. But his hope had been strong enough to create the Peace Corps out of nothing and against strong opposition, and that hopefulness had propelled him to Malaysia and into that ward.

CHAPTER 7

◇

INSTIGATOR OF HOPE

After graduating from the Potomac School in the ninth grade, I enrolled in the fall of 1979 as a sophomore at Georgetown Preparatory School. We had left Timberlawn that spring; the owner wanted to sell the entire two hundred acres, and Mom and Dad couldn't make a deal. It was an incredibly disappointing move—and to make it worse, Georgetown Prep was walking distance from Timberlawn but a forty-minute drive from our new home in Washington, D.C.

I found living in a new home and beginning in a new school very challenging, and that challenge increased when Uncle Teddy announced his presidential campaign. The campaign was an uphill battle to unseat a sitting president—Jimmy Carter—in a primary, but Teddy pushed ahead nonetheless. On weekends I would fly to cities and towns on the East Coast, sometimes meeting up with Timmy, sometimes going alone. I would leave on Friday after school and spend Saturday and Sunday at house parties, knocking on doors, and shaking as many hands as possible. On Sunday night, I would head home.

After Teddy lost, in 1980, things settled down for my junior and senior years. It was during my last two years of high school that I began to realize that Dad had habits other

fathers didn't seem to. He would slip notes under my bedroom door three or four nights a week. On note cards or
legal-sized paper, he jotted down thoughts on the dinner
conversation, his plans for the next day, or an article that he
had read that evening. And his reading habits! Whenever I
would wander into the house late on a weekend night, I
would have to walk by his room and, inevitably, I would see
the light on underneath the door. Occasionally, I would go
in to say hi and he would be propped up on his bed, reading.
And scattered all around his bed were books, magazines,
periodicals, and newspapers. He would go from one to the
other during the night, sleeping for only four to five hours.
He read *Foreign Affairs* and the Catholic magazine *America*,
the *Washington Post* and the *National Catholic Reporter*, books
on Dorothy Day and ones by Bob Woodward. Work from
the office would be stacked right next to the Baltimore Orioles yearbook. The man read everything and anything.

The pictures on his wall were also unusual. Instead of
photographs of him with powerful people, he displayed a
picture of him in his altar boy garb, with his family's parish
priest from Westminster, Maryland. Close by was a picture
of Cardinal Gibbons seated next to President Taft, with
Dad's father standing behind them. The president and cardinal were visiting the Shrivers at their Westminster home.

There was a framed picture of his mother and one of his
father. On the opposite wall, above his bureau, was a photograph of my mother—actually, three photos in a long, rectangular frame. There were scattered pictures of my siblings
or all five kids together, but those had been inserted by one
of us on the sly. If you looked good in a picture, why not
stick it in Dad's or Mom's room? Or maybe put it in front of
all the other pictures in a prominent place? It was a running
game, a joke. Kind of.

The pictures on the walls in Dad's Hyannis Port bedroom were eerily similar. Over his bed hung a framed portrait of Saint Thomas More—again, three pictures—in one long rectangular frame. Above his bureau he'd placed a framed quote from Saint Julian of Norwich: "HE said not: thou shalt not be troubled, thou shalt not be tempted, thou shalt not be distressed; but HE said: thou shalt not be overcome."

But I was only eighteen and headed to college and didn't comprehend exactly what all those books and simple photographs meant, though they were imprinted on my brain. When I entered the College of the Holy Cross in Worcester, Massachusetts, in the fall of 1982, I was sad as my mom and dad left me in my dorm room—but not that sad, for I knew I was going to see them over the Labor Day holiday in Hyannis Port just a few days later. Moments after the door to my room closed, my new roommate, Sean Duffy, who'd grown up and gone to high school in Worcester, looked at me and said, "We have to find a couch. I've got some ideas. Let's go." And out the door we went, on the first of countless adventures together. I was thrilled.

There were no Kennedy cousins nearby—as a matter of fact, I was the first male Kennedy relative to attend a Catholic college, so there was no family lineage at Holy Cross, either. And the political pressure was seemingly off; shortly after Teddy had lost in 1980, he'd made it clear that he wasn't going to run in 1984. It looked like I wouldn't have to campaign while enrolled at Holy Cross. What freedom! And though Worcester is the second-biggest city in Massachusetts, it is far enough away from the glare of the Boston media that I settled into relative anonymity quickly and easily.

That sensation didn't last long, however, for it was soon announced that Teddy would be giving a speech at Holy

Cross. If I went and he mentioned me, everyone would know that I was a freshman there; if I didn't go, what sort of a signal would that send to him? And, of course, Teddy's office knew that I was enrolled.

I hemmed and hawed. Sean told me I had to go, but somehow, on the day of the speech, Sean and I wound up shopping at a store that specialized in secondhand furnishings and clothes. I drove back to campus, covered in dust and dirt, half-hoping that I'd missed Teddy's speech, but my timing was off. I realized I still had time to make it, so I went straight to the holding room in the front of the auditorium and found myself giving Teddy a hug before he was introduced. He looked me up and down; I'm sure he was dismayed to see me in a dirty jean jacket, a ripped shirt, and jeans, though I bet he'd seen worse at a political event. He insisted that I sit on the stage while he spoke to the gathered crowd.

At a bar one night a few weeks later, some guy said to me, "Can you believe that Ted Kennedy's nephew goes to Holy Cross and came to the event in a jean jacket, looking like crap?" I guess the guy wasn't observant enough to make the connection!

But that was it. The incident never seemed to affect my professors or my friends; nor did my family name seem to impress them. They treated me just like they treated everyone else, not only that semester but throughout my four-year experience. I had walked out of the pressure cooker of the Kennedy family and into the paradise of a new group of peers. I could breathe.

Georgetown Prep and Holy Cross are both run by Catholic priests in the Society of Jesus, called Jesuits. Dad always had priests in the house, and with my budding independence and maturity, I began to develop personal relationships with the Jesuits who lived and taught on campus and led us in silent retreats. The Jesuits reminded me of my father—brainy but intellectually boisterous, tough but caring—and after all those years of grappling with the Kennedy connection, I started to thrive under their tutelage. They were faithful believers, but not pushy or showy about it. They had thought through their convictions. They didn't preach, even when they were in the pulpit at Mass. They—Father Kuzniewski and Father LaBran, Father Brooks and Father Rule—just made us think deeply and value life.

In the spring of my sophomore year, a bunch of us took a road trip to visit several of our friends who hailed from Chicago. I knew that Bobby and Maria had been born there, and I had heard that Dad had done a lot for race relations in Chicago during the 1950s, even working with Martin Luther King Jr., but that was about the extent of my knowledge, and my curiosity. Because of that Kennedy claustrophobia, or maybe by virtue of being young and self-centered, I had never had the necessary distance to gain a perspective on what Dad had done with his life.

From the moment I arrived, I felt like my friends' parents were claiming Dad as one of their own. It was the same way people in Baltimore and Westminster talked about him! His work on race and integration was the most common topic.

Later that spring, I spent some time looking into Dad's efforts in Chicago and, over years, learned more about his time there. It seemed like all the heady, international Washington stuff had clouded out his nitty-gritty accomplishments in one of America's great cities. I learned that in 1955, he was named president of the Catholic Interracial Council and, from that position, helped desegregate Chicago's Catholic high schools, considerably earlier than most cities across the country. He also pushed to eliminate segregation in Chicago's public housing and strove to end racial discrimination in Chicago's hospitals, especially the Catholic hospitals. And he worked within the Catholic Church to affect change, aligning himself with Samuel Cardinal Stritch of Chicago, an advocate of racial equality, who had been speaking out publicly against discrimination in the church and in society. In September 1956, at a Catholic Interracial Council board meeting, Cardinal Stritch praised the council for helping blacks "not in a warped spirit of condescension [that goes] slumming to the blacks" but, rather, as the publication *Catholic New World* recalled a decade later, in a way that "strives to bring men together in neighborliness."

Not everybody, however, thought so highly of the work—bricks were thrown through the windows of Dad's office at the council.

Mayor Richard J. Daley appointed Dad to be president of the Chicago Board of Education in 1955, where he spearheaded the drive to desegregate the public schools and prodded the Illinois legislature to increase pay for teachers. Dad understood and valued the importance of a top-flight education, and he said that high-quality, well-paid teachers were essential: "If Chicago is to claim credit for being the first city of our nation in any respect whatsoever, I can think of none better than being America's number one city in terms of teachers' salaries."

I also learned more about a 1960 phone call between Coretta Scott King and then–presidential candidate Jack Kennedy that likely won the election for Kennedy, helped eliminate discrimination against both Catholics and African Americans, and certainly stood out as a classic Dad story.

During the 1960 campaign, Jack and his team realized that the African American vote could be critical on Election

Day and tasked Dad with creating the civil rights division and getting out the vote.

Dad was given the job for a number of reasons, not the least of which were his strong record on civil rights issues in Chicago; his close relationships with influential Chicago congressman Williams Dawson and Louis Martin, the publisher of a chain of African American newspapers; and his friendship with Martin Luther King Jr. Dad had introduced King to a Chicago audience during the Montgomery bus boycott, for one of King's first speeches north of the Mason-Dixon Line.

The phone call took place in October 1960, just a few weeks before the presidential election. King had been jailed in Georgia for leading a sit-in at a whites-only Atlanta restaurant called the Magnolia Room. He had sat down with a group of activists and said he would keep sitting, either at the booth or in jail, until the restaurant started serving black people, too. This sparked similar sit-ins across the country, and racial tensions intensified.

Dad conspired—and, yes, I use that word intentionally—with a key aide, Harris Wofford, to get Jack to issue a statement condemning the arrests. Most of Jack's advisers wanted to placate southern governors and, as Harris recently told me, "Southern leaders and a number of northern leaders, too, told us that if Kennedy ever said anything remotely positive about Khrushchev, Jimmy Hoffa, or King, they were not going to support Kennedy." So it wasn't a complete surprise that Jack's senior advisers did not want to issue a statement or do anything regarding Dr. King's arrest.

But Dad, Wofford, and Martin—the nucleus of the civil rights division—didn't give up. Wofford and Martin came up with the idea of having Jack call Mrs. King to express his concern.

They called Dad while he was with Jack on a political trip. Dad "loved the idea," according to Wofford, who told me, "I have never met anyone in my entire life who could take an idea and make it a reality better than Sarge. He told me that he would jump in his car and drive to the hotel where Jack was and get to him before he got on the plane. And then he said, 'Bail me out of jail if I get arrested for speeding!'"

Dad found Jack in his hotel room but, as he later told Harris, "there was a big group of people in his room, and I knew that they would be opposed to the call. So I waited until they all left, one by one."

The last person in the room was Jack's longtime aide, Kenny O'Donnell. When O'Donnell went to the bathroom, Dad seized the opportunity. He suggested to Jack that he call Mrs. King to express his concerns about her husband's safety. After a brief discussion, Jack agreed to make the call. "How do I get her on the phone?" Jack asked. Dad pulled Mrs. King's number out of his pocket and handed it to him. Jack asked him to dial the number, as he had to pack to catch a flight. Dad dialed, and Mrs. King and Jack talked for a little over a minute; Jack didn't mention endorsements or the election but simply extended his best wishes to her and Dr. King. The call was over before O'Donnell got out of the bathroom. He quickly figured out that something had happened and told Dad that he had probably cost Kennedy the election. When the other senior advisers found out about the call later that day, all hell broke loose. The civil rights division was closed immediately.

But the key breakthrough came when Martin Luther King Sr., often called Daddy King, learned about the call. King had long been considered anti-Catholic and had even signed a newspaper ad endorsing Nixon, clearly because Nixon was a Protestant. But Jack's call to his son's wife suddenly and wholly enlightened him, and he publicly praised

Jack. He endorsed my uncle days later, saying, "I had expected to vote against Senator Kennedy because of his religion. But now he can be my president. If Kennedy has the courage to wipe the tears from Coretta's eyes, [I] will vote for him whatever his religion."

The question then became how to spread the King endorsement across the country. Martin could put it in his newspapers, but they would be released just a few days before the election, and that might be too late.

Martin considered publishing and distributing a pamphlet but was worried that the campaign would reject it, having just closed down its civil rights division. Martin called Dad and outlined his idea about the pamphlet. Dad came up with a plan of action: don't publish anything new, just publish statements made by Martin Luther King Sr. and other African American leaders. "You don't need to ask Bobby's permission," he told Martin. "Let's do it. If it works, he'll like it. If we don't do it, and we don't get enough Negro votes, he and Jack wouldn't like that, and we would all be kicking ourselves for a long time."

The pamphlet, *The Case of Martin Luther King,* was officially sponsored by the Freedom Crusade Committee (which was composed of two ministers). It included quotes from Martin Luther King Jr., Mrs. King, Daddy King, and several other prominent African American leaders, including Ralph David Abernathy. As Wofford recounted in his 1980 memoir *Of Kennedys and Kings,* Abernathy said:

> I earnestly and sincerely feel that it is time for all of us to take off our Nixon buttons. Senator Kennedy did something great and wonderful when he personally called Coretta King. . . . Since Mr. Nixon has been silent through all this, I am going to return his silence when I go to the voting booth.

By October 30, Dad had printed fifty thousand copies and mailed them all over the country. He then printed an additional quarter of a million in Chicago; these were distributed in African American churches across Illinois and Wisconsin. The feedback was so strong that Dad ordered more, and by Sunday, November 6, two million copies had been circulated.

The results were stunning: on Election Day, seven out of ten African American voters pulled the Kennedy lever, and the African American vote was a larger proportion of overall votes than in any previous election. As Wofford recalled, James Michener later wrote that the call and the follow-up afterward were "the single event which came closest to being the one vital accident of the campaign. In doing this, [Kennedy] did not lose Georgia or South Carolina or Texas. Instead he won the Negro vote in New York and Chicago and Philadelphia, and thus the Presidency."

Some have said that the call was a brilliant political move, designed to swing critical votes to Kennedy, but I believe that Dad's primary motivator was his abiding devotion to a Judeo-Christian vision of hope. That same motivation had made him bring the crucifix that he had laid on Jack's coffin to Rome to be blessed by the pope and then, days later, by the head of the Greek Orthodox Church, even though the two leaders had not interacted for centuries.

Yes, Dad was a political animal, and I had the capacity in my genes to be one, too. Even at age nineteen, I fancied a future for myself in the same line of accomplishment as great men like MLK and JFK and Dad, because that is how Kennedys were supposed to see themselves.

But for Dad, the fulfillment of the duty to hope was more important than winning and ruling; the service to hopefulness trumped the office every time, even though the offices he held made for a sparkling résumé.

It took me until after his death to see it clearly: his faith demanded his hopefulness, and his hope underpinned his work. He worked to give others the opportunity to hope—that was his abiding ambition.

LOVE

Without love, which really is respect for your fellow man, there can be no faith in ourselves, or in others. Without faith, there can be no hope; without hope, there's no future. . . .

—SARGENT SHRIVER, Winter Convocation at Wilberforce University, January 25, 1968

◇

CHAPTER 8

SOMETHING SPECIAL

Mom and Dad were not fans of public displays of affection. In fact, quite the contrary. Sometimes at Dad's family birthday parties, my brothers, sister, and I would chant for Mom to "Kiss him! Kiss him!" We'd continue chanting until they smooched, at which we'd all roar with laughter.

Dad would go for a hug and Mom would shout, "Don't do that, Sargie! You know how I hate to be tickled." We'd chant again, "Kiss him! Kiss him!" They would smooch again, and the yelling in the room would grow even louder.

Their marriage flourished for fifty-six years, but it happened only after seven years of courtship!

After the war, Dad got a job at a law firm, but he couldn't stand it; he then went to work for *Newsweek* magazine as a junior editor. It was 1946, and Dad claimed he was out and about all the time. "I had a lot of girlfriends," he'd laugh when asked what life was like after World War II in New York City.

"Oh, Sargie," Mom would say, "you were attractive, but I don't think you had *that many girlfriends*."

"Oh, yes, I did, Eunie baby. I just didn't tell you about all of them!"

He did have an active enough social life that he was

invited to a party where he met Mom. Dad knew her brother Jack—they'd gone to high school together at the Canterbury School for a year, before Jack transferred—and he knew Mom's older sister Kathleen, who was best friends with one of Dad's "girlfriends."

Dad asked Mom out shortly after they met. "It was love at first sight for me," he said, "but it took your mother a while longer to fall for me."

A few days after their first date, he got a call from Grandpa Kennedy, who asked Dad to meet him at his hotel for breakfast.

"I was scared, to say the least, when he called," Dad recollected. "I didn't know if I had upset your mother—why would Joe Kennedy call me, a junior guy at *Newsweek*? He was one of the richest, most powerful men in America.

"I went to the meeting and he asked me to read his son Joe's letters to see if they could be published. At our next meeting, I told him I didn't think they were good enough."

A few days later, Grandpa called again, this time to offer Dad a job. At first Dad didn't know whether to accept it, but eventually the allure of working for Joe Kennedy (and maybe getting to know his daughter better) convinced him to say yes.

Although Mom and Dad went on a few more dates in New York City, sparks hadn't started flying. Not yet.

Soon thereafter, Grandpa moved Dad to Chicago to help manage his newest acquisition, the Merchandise Mart, which at the time was the largest commercial building in the world. Meanwhile, Mom moved to Washington to work for the Justice Department. She shared a house in Georgetown with Jack, who had just been elected to Congress. After a few months, Grandpa called Dad and told him to head to D.C. to help Mom, who was the head of a new entity called the Committee on Juvenile Delinquency.

For the next year, Mom and Dad worked side by side in the Justice Department. Dad loved to tell stories about how hard they worked and how Mom would kiss him only once or twice a day! After a year, however, they both resigned; Dad went back to Chicago, while Mom moved to New York. Although Mom relocated to Chicago in 1950, their romance was not serious.

But politics played a hand in uniting them. When Uncle Jack decided to run for Senate in 1952, Mom moved to Massachusetts to help the cause, and Grandpa again transferred Dad. This time, Dad headed to Boston, where he lived with Grandma and Grandpa in their apartment during the campaign. After Uncle Jack's surprising victory, Dad returned to Chicago. Mom joined him there in late 1952, and just a few months later they became engaged. It had taken seven years for Dad's dream—to be engaged to Mom—to come true. During those seven years, his hope sustained his love, or vice versa.

When Mom died, Maria gave the eulogy, and she described their relationship perfectly: "She had a husband who was devoted to her in every sense of that word. A man who marveled at everything she said and did. He didn't mind if her hair was a mess, if she beat him at tennis, or challenged his ideas. He let her rip, he let her roar—and he loved it."

Today it may not seem like that big a deal for a man to let a woman rip or roar, but back then it was. Let's not forget that the role of women in the 1950s and 1960s was much more limited than it is today. There had been only two female Cabinet members ever, and no female Supreme Court justices; there wasn't even a women's professional tennis circuit!

My father wasn't threatened by a strong woman who wanted to turn convention on its head by fighting for the rights of people with developmental disabilities—not an obvious or popular cause when she championed it. In fact, at the time, most people with developmental disabilities were hidden from society, often locked away in institutions. But Mom was a force of nature. She focused like a laser beam on helping people with developmental disabilities experience all of life's richness. She worked tirelessly and furiously to pull them out of the shadows and into the sunshine. She didn't care that so-called experts told her that "the retarded" couldn't swim, couldn't catch a ball, couldn't play a team sport, couldn't socialize. She told all those experts that they were wrong, and she fought like hell to prove it.

Dad embraced Mom and her ideas; he let her rip and roar because he loved her. To many people—men in particular—Dad may have appeared weak standing next to and often behind such a well-known and powerful woman, or too deferential to Mom's ideas, to her personality. But Dad, "a husband who was devoted to her in every sense of that word," was in love, and love demanded nothing short of that devotion.

Though the results of that devotion may have unsettled some people, it transformed the lives of many more. Mom organized the first International Special Olympics Summer Games in Chicago in July 1968, but that gathering was hardly what the games would become in later years. A thousand athletes from twenty-six states and Canada appeared at those games, with only a scattering of fans in a nearly deserted Soldier Field stadium.

When Mom returned to Paris (where Dad was now the ambassador) after the games, she decided that people with developmental disabilities should be invited to the U.S. embassy to participate in sports training.

In the embassy itself.

Frances Cook, who worked for Dad at the time, remembers it clearly:

> You know those big tires? How athletes try to improve
> their quickness by hopping through about twenty of

them lined up alongside each other? Mrs. Shriver lined
those up in the dining room of the U.S. embassy. The
kids would train in there, while others would train outside, running through obstacle courses and participating
in other athletic drills. They would rotate around and
your mother would also get into the swimming pool to
adjust the athletes' techniques, but she had to travel to a
pool that was close to Versailles. The French didn't know
quite what to make of the whole scene.

"I will never forget overhearing a phone conversation
that an embassy staffer was having," Dad told me more than
once. "The gentleman was talking in French and didn't realize I could understand it. He said, 'These Shrivers are crazy!
They've rolled up the carpets for these retarded children
and they're running all over the place. They have hired the
retarded to work here in the embassy. They are working
right here in the United States embassy alongside us—the
retarded! Alongside us! *Mon Dieu!*'" Dad let out a belly laugh
every time he told that story. "Your mother had so much
energy, and the embassy was alive. It was terrific!"

Even today not many ambassadors would invite people
with developmental disabilities to run around a U.S. embassy.
But my mother and father were convinced that if people with
developmental disabilities were welcomed in the American
embassy, it would impress not only the other diplomats but
also the French people. It's no wonder that France was one
of the first countries to create a Special Olympics program;
no wonder that when my parents left their post, Charles de
Gaulle, the father of a child with developmental disabilities
and no fan of America, sent so many flowers to the embassy
that one man alone couldn't carry them.

Mom and Dad's marriage was not built just around creating movements like the Peace Corps and Special Olympics,

or their work together on the Committee on Juvenile Delinquency and political campaigns. They loved to play sports together, and they devised plenty of other crazy activities. After McDonald's signed on as a corporate sponsor for Special Olympics—a major show of support for the organization— Dad somehow convinced his contacts at McDonald's to send Ronald McDonald to Hyannis Port for Mom's sixty-first birthday. Yes, Ronald McDonald, the clown.

It was a surprise party, and Mom was definitely surprised when she walked into the dining room and saw Ronald McDonald there, along with Big Macs and french fries in bags! Uncle Teddy almost fell on the floor. "Well, this might take the cake, Sarge!" he bellowed as he walked into the room. "Eunie's birthday party with Big Macs, fries, and wine. Wow!" I ended up corresponding with Ronald McDonald, who was an avid baseball fan.

And there was the party they had after leaving Paris.

Dad arrived home from work one afternoon to find the backyard at Timberlawn filled with people with developmental disabilities engaged in various physical activities. That was not unusual. Camp Shriver was in full bloom at that time. Inside the house, Dad saw food and drinks everywhere. He took a sip of the punch; he thought there was a strange taste to it, so he asked one of the volunteers what was in it. The volunteer told him that it had been made in the kitchen, so Dad headed there and found several empty wine bottles. Mom had told the volunteers to grab some wine and put it in the punch to give it a little extra kick. Unfortunately, they'd used what was closest, which were the bottles President de Gaulle had given my parents when they'd left Paris! I can't remember the vintage, but Dad always said that it was the best wine ever made, and that this was the only time he ever got mad at Mom.

Mom always denied that she knew it had happened, but

you could tell by the look in her eye and the smile on her face that she understood a little bit more than she was willing to admit. Whenever the story was told, Dad would sigh at the end and say, "If only I could have tried a glass of that wine . . ."

When I gave my eulogy for Dad, I wrote about his love affair with my mom:

> And perhaps the most beautiful sunrise that he created, a
> sunrise that will never set, was his marriage to the woman
> of his dreams. He loved Mummy like crazy for fifty-six
> years. You know that look a man has when he looks at a
> woman that he really loves? Daddy looked at Mummy
> that way, every day. When you are loved that way, you
> are so confident and happy—no wonder that, together,
> they did so much.

I don't know how else to describe "that look" other than as the way my father always looked not only at my mother but at each of his children every day. As a young boy who would struggle through his adolescence, I knew that look and understood that, regardless of any obstacles I might face, an incredible foundation of love and support was there for me. It was that look, that love, that sustained me even as I was overwhelmed by the burdens of my identity and family expectations. If love is generosity, utter selflessness, and if a look can show that sort of love, then that is what his gaze accomplished.

He looked at Mom as his bride but also, I believe, as a gift from God to him. He loved her in this sacred vein. His gaze was holy. If there was a spot in which faith and hope and love connected for Dad, it was in that space in which his gaze beheld his wife. That gaze said what he wrote to her in a letter once:

I want you to have in writing something I have told you often: you have meant and shall always mean more to me than any other human being. If I end up in heaven someday with our most precious Lord and Savior, you my courageous and wise wife will be the single most important reason for my being there. Second only to our Lord himself, you will have saved my soul—by your intelligence, your example, your dedication to our Lord and to the Blessed Mother, by your faith and by your love.

◇

CHAPTER 9

TOP MAN

Dad had another lifelong love—actually, a friendship as deep and rich as any I have ever seen. If Mom was the constant coconspirator in everything Dad did, then Richard Franklin Ragsdale (known to everyone he met simply as "Rags") was the loyal lieutenant.

Rags started working for Dad two weeks before I was born. He was with the federal government at the time, serving as a jack-of-all-trades, running errands for big-shot government officials, when he was assigned to be Dad's driver. "Rags is the best driver in Washington, D.C.," Dad said countless times. "He weaves and ducks through traffic better than any human being has ever done it. He'll cut a car off every now and then, but he never gets in a crash and he has never caused one. He's a master behind the wheel."

In practically no time Rags proved himself invaluable on a variety of fronts, and before long he was working for my mom and dad full-time, adding his own brand of stability to the chaos of our hectic house.

In many ways, Rags was a walking contradiction. His seemingly serious, gruff exterior belied his warm and affectionate nature. He was fluent in all manner of curse words and had an Irish gift for hilariously inappropriate tall tales.

He griped almost incessantly about the paces my parents put him through—and yet he was the most intensely loyal and relentlessly hardworking person I've ever known.

He was five foot eight, with a solid build, creased skin that seemed perpetually tanned, and thick, wavy hair—which he always claimed had turned gray because of my mother. A veteran of World War II, he'd fought under General Patton, an experience he sometimes maintained had been more enjoyable than his employment with our family was. "Goddamn, Markie," he'd say, "your mother is working my ass to the bone!"

Rags's unfiltered language always made me feel a little more grown-up, like he was talking to me as if I were a man instead of a child. But that was simply a reflection of how uniquely genuine a person Rags was. It didn't matter your age or position or lot in life; with Rags, what you saw was what you got. No filter, no pretense, no airs, and no judgment. Not with Rags.

Dad loved this about him, their uncomplicated views of human nature surprisingly simpatico. Ultimately, Dad came to rely on Rags, both as a man who could help him get things done and as a trusted friend and companion. Dad called Rags "Top Man."

They were from similar worlds in some respects: Dad, German-Irish, born and raised in western Maryland and Baltimore, lived most of his life in suburban Maryland; Rags, Irish with, as he always said, "some Cherokee blood in me," was born and raised in Washington, D.C., and lived the vast majority of his life in suburban Maryland as well. They were both brought up as devout Catholics by families who barely survived the Depression. Both men volunteered to fight in World War II and survived brutal combat.

In countless other ways, they made an odd pairing. Dad had gone to prestigious institutions, including Canterbury

School, Yale College, and Yale Law School while Rags's education came from the U.S. Army infantry ("My degree is the shrapnel in my ass, Markie"). After the war, Dad went to work for one of the most powerful, richest men in America; Rags got a job with the post office. Dad was a natural statesman who expanded the thinking of the country, its leaders, and the next generation about issues like social justice, racial equality, and economic opportunity; Rags was always close to political power but never presumed that he could influence it.

Despite their differences, Dad and Rags were inseparable best friends. More than one person over the years compared Dad and Rags's relationship to an off-kilter version of Morgan Freeman and Jessica Tandy in the movie *Driving Miss Daisy*. To Rags and Dad, arguing, bickering, and griping with each other was a form of sport that went hand in hand with their intense mutual devotion and loyalty.

In retrospect, Rags's loyalty to my father was mind-blowing, even if it was masked by typical Rags sarcasm or halfhearted complaints. On more than one occasion, at the end of a long day, Rags told me, "Markie, your damn parents are driving me nuts, running me in a million different directions. I gotta take you to school in D.C., pick up your father at the airport, get your mother's medicine in Rockville, take Anthony to the doctor, and Bobby is arriving at National Airport at ten tonight. Shit, man, I've had it! I'm a goddamn fool if I take any more of their craziness!" The next morning, he would arrive at the house before six, and you could hear Dad and Rags banging around the kitchen before piling into the car and heading out to seven o'clock Mass. Together.

For almost forty years, they were together for, on average, six days a week. And that daily morning Mass was the beginning ritual of their day. They attended Mass together

on thousands of occasions. While Dad read Jacques Mari-
tain, Hans Küng, Pierre Teilhard de Chardin, Dorothy Day,
and many others, Rags read just the Bible. But the constant
and regular physical act of attending Mass together, receiv-
ing the Eucharist together, and exchanging the sign of peace
with each other made their bond deep and personal.

Other than that early-morning routine, however, no two
days were the same during Rags's tenure with our family.
For all those years, he showed up at our house and tackled
whatever the day demanded. And with five growing kids
and parents who thrived on using our home as ground zero
for their countless initiatives, campaigns, and projects, whatever the day demanded usually meant far more than any one
person could reasonably be expected to manage. Somehow,
Rags held it all together.

A typical day (if there ever was such a thing) looked something like this: Rags would arrive in the predawn hours,
meet Dad, drive to Mass, and get home in time to make us
kids breakfast. He would drop us off at school if Dad couldn't
do it that day, then race back to our home in suburban Maryland, where buses would be unloading dozens of children
and young adults with intellectual disabilities for the sports
camps my mother organized in our yard. He'd arrive just in
time to yell at the bus driver, who inevitably would have
driven across the yard and crushed some tender shrubs that
had been put in the week before, under Rags's instruction.
With the pool full of Special Olympics athletes and volunteer
coaches, the pool pump would break, Mom would blame
Rags, and he'd blame the pool-repair guy, whom he'd call,
instructing the fellow to "get your ass over here quick because
Mrs. Shriver is hot!"

He'd then start barking orders at the shell-shocked cook,
who hadn't known that there would be forty or so athletes—
all hungry from a morning full of sports—for lunch. Rags

would help the cook, and before you knew it enough chicken salad sandwiches (his specialty) and potato salad for a small army would be out on the patio. After ensuring that the pool guy wasn't making things any worse, he'd race to pick up some or all of my siblings and me from school, dropping some of us off at after-school events along the way. Every time he picked me up from school, we would stop at Baskin-Robbins or Gifford's Ice Cream store for a treat. Rags always advocated for a more generous serving, telling the server, "Shit, man, these are hungry kids—you'd better give them a bigger scoop than that!"

With our cones piled high, we'd load ourselves back into the car and head home, where a note would be on the door, written in my mother's hard-to-decipher chicken scratch, letting Rags know that our parish priest was coming to dinner and that Dad needed to be home early. So he'd kick us out of the car and fly downtown at breakneck speed. At the office, Dad's longtime assistant, Jeannie Main, would tell Rags that Dad had taken a cab to Capitol Hill but had not mentioned whom he was meeting. Rags would drive to the Capitol and, after much yelling and cursing and harassing of others, he'd somehow manage to track Dad down and get him back out to the house just in time for dinner. While dinner was being served, Rags would go out to check on the pool pump, which the repair guy hadn't been able to fix; he'd break out his tools and get it running himself.

Then he'd do it all again the next day, with a different cast of characters but always the same level of chaos.

My siblings and I didn't make life easier for Rags, either. Once, a new couple, hired as a cook and housekeeper, moved into the house with their young son. They'd been on the job for only a few days before Anthony pushed their boy into the pond in our backyard. The child was scared out of his wits, and his enraged father, the cook, proceeded to chase

Anthony around the yard with a butcher knife. Rags saved the day, jumping on the guy while Anthony ran to his room, where he hid until the family packed up and left that same night.

And there was the time a friend started the go-kart before anyone was behind the wheel. The machine had a high idle and sped off, straight into the pool. It took Rags a couple of hours to get it out, but he did.

The pergola in the front yard had vines and flowers growing all over it. Rags put a Santa Claus and reindeer set on top of the pergola one Christmas, and there it sat for years. "I'm not taking it down," Rags told me. "It was too much damn work getting it up, and I'm not going to do it every year." The excitement and joy of Christmas seemed to happen every day at Timberlawn, and Santa and his reindeer only reinforced it.

But it was mainly my parent's nonstop swirl of activities that made things so chaotic for Rags. As a boy, I found it a fun environment to grow up in, even if I didn't fully appreciate the social movement behind all the activity. When my parents threw a "Farm Worker Fiesta" with César Chávez, it was like a big picnic. When Special Olympics camps were held, Mom would recruit big-time athletes like Rocky Bleier and Rafer Johnson to come out and help promote what she was doing. We'd run around during fund-raisers for senators or congressmen, having a good time even if the speeches fell on deaf ears.

I doubt that many of the people who attended those events paid much attention to Rags. But he, as much as anyone, was responsible for their success. He kept things running smoothly, or at least as smoothly as was humanly possible.

He worked alongside Dad during the War on Poverty days and went to Paris when Dad became ambassador. His wife, Elaine, and one of his children, Kristie, joined him there.

When we returned to Maryland, at the end of March 1970, Rags was right back at Timberlawn.

Shortly thereafter, Dad started going around the state of Maryland, talking to people about a potential run for governor. Again, Rags was right there.

Marvin Mandel had been elected governor by the Maryland General Assembly in January 1969, replacing Spiro Agnew, who had run for vice president with Richard Nixon in 1968. The election for a new governor was in November 1970. Dad told me later, "Something just felt strange to me. I couldn't put my finger on it. People told me not to run against a powerful sitting Democratic governor. I always felt that something more was going on."

By all accounts, Dad struggled with the decision of whether to run for too long, and his fledgling campaign grew disorganized and fell apart. Dad was also right that something was off with the Mandel administration.

Mandel was indicted and convicted of mail fraud in 1977, though his conviction was vacated in 1988 because the Supreme Court, in another case, had found the law under which Mandel was convicted unconstitutional.

After the aborted run, Dad focused his time on helping congressional Democrats succeed in the November 1970 elections. House majority leader Carl Albert and Senate majority leader Mike Mansfield announced that Dad would lead a new organization called Congressional Leadership for the Future. The organization helped the Democrats succeed in the 1970 election, setting the stage for the 1972 presidential election.

When George McGovern won the Democratic primary for president, he wanted Uncle Teddy to run as his vice president, but Teddy said no. McGovern then selected Missouri senator Thomas Eagleton as his running mate. Within days, the ticket was in trouble—Eagleton had had three experiences with psychiatric treatment. Though McGovern initially supported him, Eagleton was forced out days after accepting the nomination. After the Eagleton debacle, Teddy again refused McGovern's invitation; so did a number of other potential candidates, including Maine senator Edmund Muskie. Muskie dragged his decision out in public over a couple of days, further damaging McGovern's candidacy. Dad was, by some accounts, the seventh choice; nonetheless, on August 5 he accepted the invitation.

In his acceptance speech on national television, Dad said, "I am not embarrassed to be George McGovern's seventh choice for vice president. We Democrats may be short of money. We're not short of talent. Ted Kennedy, Ed Muskie, Hubert Humphrey, Abe Ribicoff, Tom Eagleton—what a galaxy of stars. Pity Mr. Nixon—his first and only choice was Spiro Agnew."

Dad was proud to be McGovern's running mate; he always claimed that seven was his favorite number. In fact, he called our immediate family the "lucky seven," telling us that he was the luckiest man alive to have five healthy kids and a loving wife. When he bought a new motorboat the year after the campaign, he named it the Lucky Seven.

When he accepted the nomination, I was eight years old, running around Hyannis Port, swimming, playing softball, and riding my bike. All of a sudden, there was more action than normal at the house. Serious-looking, tall men driving black cars arrived to protect my father, and all sorts of people descended on the house. A few days later, Dad left to campaign.

The campaign was short-lived. I never went on the campaign plane or bus, but I remember Rags driving us to a nearby neighborhood, handing Anthony and me leaflets, and telling us to start knocking on doors. It didn't go so well. A few folks graciously accepted our material, but the doors slammed in my face are etched in my memory. I was a third grader at Mater Dei School and remember being teased by a few classmates, who said my father was going to lose.

And they were right. Just three months later, the McGovern-Shriver ticket suffered a landslide defeat, of a magnitude unseen in American political history. They won only Massachusetts and Washington, D.C. Rags didn't leave after that campaign; he stayed with Mom and Dad, day in and day out, for most of the next thirty years.

Ten years later, when I was a high school senior, Rags took me on another trip, a short one to our local post office. I had to register for the draft, and even though I had a driver's license, he insisted on taking me. The registry was something President Carter had initiated—the government wanted a database of all American male citizens because the geopolitical climate had made war, especially nuclear war, suddenly plausible and more terrifying than ever before. I had intended to go myself for weeks but had procrastinated to the point that Rags realized it. There was something else going on, though, something someone my age usually lacks the emotional antennae to recognize. But as I reflect, I am more aware than ever of how silent, almost solemn Rags was during that ten-minute drive.

Dad had been spearheading the no-first-strike movement over the previous several months. Nuclear-proliferation experts, diplomatic big shots, and all sorts of politicians had been converging on our house to hammer out a policy statement against nuclear war. It was 1982, and fear of the Soviet Union drove much of the political dialogue. I noticed an even more acute level of intensity around the house during those months, and those dinner meetings must have touched Rags, too.

I loved him like a second father, and I knew he loved me like a son, even though he rarely showed it; and I could tell that he wanted to make this trip with me for some reason. As we left the post office, Rags put his arm around me for about ten seconds, which was five seconds longer than he had ever done before. His gestures of affection were usually a yell or a gentle shove. All he said was "Good job, Markie. Hope the draft never happens."

We got back into the car, he drove me to the house, and I can feel his arm around my shoulder to this day.

I always loved the fact that Dad—a "great man" in so many people's eyes—had a best friend like Rags. As his wife, Elaine, told me, "Your dad was very, very fond of Richard, and Richard loved your dad like a brother." She was right. They say you can judge a person by their friends. I always knew that Dad and Rags were best friends, but it wasn't until their last years together that I would understand the depth of their relationship.

◇

CHAPTER 10

LOVE IN ACTION

The stands in the football stadium at Louisiana State University that July in 1983 were bouncing up and down. As Dad and I entered the stadium, the LSU mascot, a Bengal tiger, growled at us from its cage. We had walked through the parking lot, which smelled like all those vowely sounding, spice-filled foods people in Louisiana eat—Creole cooking, jambalaya, gumbo. We were there for the opening of the 6th International Special Olympics Summer Games, and it seemed like Bourbon Street had simply upped and moved to Baton Rouge for the night. Dad and Mom were beaming at the spectacle—more than sixty-five thousand people celebrating the talents of those whom society had for so long ignored.

I was going to march into the stadium with the delegation of Maryland athletes within the U.S. team, and as Dad left me, he looked over and said, "Enjoy the party!"

When we proceeded in, the place went wild at the sight of the American team; I understood clearly then that these were Dad's favorite parties—not bashes at the Democratic convention, not highbrow festivities in Paris, not Kennedy clambakes on the Cape or Shriver reunions in Union

Mills. At these Special Olympics events, he could let go, forget himself, dive into the crowd, and love life in all its variety.

Dad became president of Special Olympics in 1984 when he officially left the law firm of Fried, Frank, Harris, Shriver, and Kampelman. Before too long, he was leading the charge to expand Special Olympics programs all across the world. I suspect the mischievous side of him just wanted to keep having parties like the one at LSU, but a deeper motivator was obviously in play. Everyone had always joked that Mom was the boss; now it was a fact. And Dad loved it!

In November 1985, Dad led a delegation of Special Olympics staff to visit China, Japan, and South Korea. He was accompanied by Tom Songster, the director of sports, and Jamie Kirkpatrick, the director of International Programs for Special Olympics. They were met by Dicken Yung, the chairman of Special Olympics Hong Kong, and Anna Tam, the sports director of Special Olympics Hong Kong, which was still a British colony.

Dad wanted to coax China into the Special Olympics movement and believed that the best way to facilitate the relationship was by inviting a team of officials and athletes to attend the 3rd International Special Olympics Winter Games in Park City, Utah, in March 1985. At that point in time, as Tom Songster told me, "Everything was pretty closed in China. They didn't have a Special Olympics program. They had just joined the Olympic movement in 1980 at the Winter Games and participated in their first Summer Games in 1984."

China was slowly, begrudgingly, starting to acknowledge that people with intellectual disabilities even existed. Dad had arranged a series of meetings and visits, including one to an institution in Beijing. As Songster told me:

Your father thrived in that setting. It was a well-organized facility. It was very medical-looking—everyone wore white coats, and there were people with physical and mental disabilities throughout the building, but it looked like they were getting services. You have to remember that this was the place the government wanted us to see. They toured us all around the building and then brought us all to a courtyard out back, where Sarge participated in a spoon-egg race with children with developmental disabilities. He took off his coat, smiled, and laughed and started to run with the spoon in his hand. Before he got ten yards, he dropped the egg, and everyone laughed and he had to run back and get another. He lost the race. The Chinese officials were delighted, and the state-run media covering the event were delighted as well.

Dad had also arranged to meet Deng Pufang, the son of the then-paramount leader of the People's Republic of China, Deng Xiaoping.

In 1968, at the age of twenty-four, Deng Pufang had been thrown out of a window of a three-story building at Beijing University by his father's political enemies. Refused immediate medical care, he'd been partially paralyzed. It was during one of his visits for medical care to Hong Kong that he'd met Dicken Yung.

Dad and Deng Pufang hit it off immediately. According to Songster, "Sarge told him that China needed to recognize Special Olympics. He said that China had the largest population and was one of the most important countries in the world and that Special Olympics needed to be part of it all." Dad's persuasive message resonated with Chinese officials. China sent an official delegation—three "observers" and no athletes—to those 1985 games.

In 1987, China dispatched its first official team delegation to the 7th International Special Olympics games at the University of Notre Dame. Dad worked tirelessly over the next fifteen years, meeting with Chinese officials in the United States and China in an effort to convince them to fully accept the Special Olympics movement.

Eventually, Dad's dream of having China host an international competition came true. In 2007, the 12th Special Olympics World Summer Games were held in Shanghai. More than seventy-five hundred athletes from 164 countries participated, and the opening ceremony was attended by eighty thousand people. Unfortunately, Dad was too sick to travel, but today Special Olympics China is the largest program in the world.

When he made that groundbreaking trip to China, I was studying, and probably partying a bit too much, at Holy Cross. I knew he was there; he called me a few times from China, and the buzz and static on the line were so heavy it sounded like he was calling from Mars. But he said, "I love you." I always heard those words loud and clear from whatever backwater village or bustling capital he said them to me.

So often when he was making history, I was unaware of it at the time. I guess that is how it goes with our parents— we are self-preoccupied and busy, and we don't realize until later just what they achieved with their lives.

One day, I would understand the gravity of that China trip in all its glory. Six months after Dad's death I would be sitting in Athens, Greece, the home of the Olympics, watching the opening ceremonies for the 13th Special Olympics World Summer Games. And I would think back to the smell of gumbo and the roar of the caged tiger and the rocking stadium at LSU. I would imagine the meetings he had in China, his insistence and guile all put toward improving

the lives of millions of Chinese people who had been exiled
or ignored or worse, simply because they had been dealt
a different genetic hand at birth. And I would grasp that
unique devotion—quite simply, that hope and love—he
summoned for everything he undertook, particularly when
it involved the powerless.

FATHERHOOD

The pressures we all live under are getting so furious that it's more of a challenge to be a responsible bread-winner and a responsible father at the same time. . . . It is a battle . . . to raise children these days, in the old traditions and values. It's a battle to keep them from absorbing the cynicism, the negative attitudes that were born out of the cold war, and are now, like smog and fallout, part of our atmosphere. . . . It's not your accomplishments, or your annuities but your attitudes that shape the lifelong attitudes of your children. And I don't think I'm the father of this or any year unless my children grow up with some sense of commitment and hopefulness about the problems of our age.

—Sargent Shriver, accepting the
Father of the Year Award,
New York City,
May 28, 1964

◇

CHAPTER 11

A GOOD FATHER'S LOVE

Dad's innumerable accomplishments on the world's great
stage sometimes overwhelmed my recognition of the
good things he achieved in the role that mattered to him
most—as our father. This came hurtling home to me soon
after his funeral when I finally read, word for word, a story
I had heard countless times.

Dad had recently returned from France, where he had
been the U.S. ambassador and, at just about the worst time
imaginable, he learned that my brother Bobby had been
arrested for possession of marijuana.

At Dad's funeral, Bobby told the story:

I was sixteen years old in 1970 and I got into serious
trouble. I was arrested for smoking marijuana. . . . A lot
of police officers came to our house in Hyannis Port and
served arrest warrants on my cousin and me.

Prior to that moment, I was a normal sixteen-year-old
boy. I had my Beatles and Stones records. I was mad at my
mother, who told me I couldn't go to Woodstock because
I was too young. I had a crush on a neighborhood girl
who never noticed me. I tried so hard to be cool, and I
knew deep in my heart that I was not cool at all.

I was very aware of the Kennedy family position, and more than a little scared about it. Uncle Bobby had died in 1968, and Uncle Jack only seven years before. Uncle Teddy's name was everywhere as a candidate for president in 1972. I was terrified that he, too, would be shot by some madman.

More than anything, as Timmy said, I wanted to be a man, so I could help, but I was a boy.

So being arrested for drugs, witnessing the arrival of a thousand journalists at our door—it's hard to believe, but it's really true—and seeing the story on the front page of the *New York Times,* above the fold, was an enormous personal failure, a complete humiliation, public humiliation, in all the obvious ways, private humiliation, in a very deep way.

I let my family down; I dishonored my father's name, and my mother's name. In the house, before Daddy arrived, the lawyers came and went. A barber arrived and cut my long, cool hair to a crew cut—Mummy supervised that. There were many disapproving looks, and it was a rough period.

Then Daddy arrived and told me to come into his room. It was a very, very long walk to his room. He sat me down on the edge of his bed, pulled up a chair, looked me right in the eye, and said:

"Listen, you are a good kid. Don't listen to anybody else. I'm your father, and I am going to take care of you. Do you understand me?"

"Yes, sir," I said.

And that was it—no moralizing, no criticizing. I went back to my room and knew I was safe. And so it was.

The next day we went to court, were charged and released to our parents' custody. Dad took me to the airport; we flew to California. We played tennis eight hours a day, in very hot sun, went to bed at eight-thirty, up at six-thirty, on the court at seven-thirty. I felt safe, and stayed in California for a month.

This is the story of my father saving my life. Of how I always saw manliness and strength.

It's a sad story because I know many boys and many girls have many moments like this in their lives, but they don't have a dad like my father and they have to struggle without the strength of such a person. I hope you feel, in the telling of my story today, some of the overwhelming gratitude I felt that day for my father. I say good-bye to him today with that gratitude very deeply and strongly in my heart.

Bobby did not mention the statement Dad issued at the time of the incident, published in full by the *New York Times*:

We are deeply distressed to learn that our son Bobby has been charged with the possession of marijuana last month in Hyannis. He has never been involved in any such situation before, and we trust that he never will be again.

If he has done anything wrong, we are sure he will make reparations in a manly and courageous manner. We love him, and for all of his 16 years he has been a joy and a pride to us.

We will help him in every way to re-establish his sense of responsibility for himself and for others, his dedication to high ideals, his personal self-confidence and dignity.

Young people today are being subjected to the most profound temptations and stresses. All young persons, especially at this moment our son and all other youngsters arrested with him, have our deepest sympathy.

We ask for human understanding for our son's plight,
and we pray that God will help him and all the other
boys and girls involved.

When I reread the statement recently, the word "manly"
seemed out of place. I don't ever recall Dad telling me to
"act more like a man." Why did he write that in 1970?

And then I noticed that Bobby described Dad's behavior
during this experience as conveying "manliness and strength."

I called Bobby and asked him if he had read Dad's statement to the press while preparing his eulogy. He had not, he
told me. I asked him if Dad had ever told him to "act like a
man," especially during those difficult days. "No, he didn't,"
Bobby said. "He didn't even yell at me during the whole
thing."

I read him Daddy's press statement and the line from his
own eulogy and there was silence on the phone. "I have to
think about why I used that word," Bobby said.

Was the use of the word purely coincidental? At first I
thought so, but then I saw it as entirely appropriate. Dad loved
us aggressively, bigheartedly, unconditionally. He didn't see
the role of a father as a tough guy yelling at his kids, intimi-
dating them with a firm and unrelenting hand. That's not
the way Dad acted when Bobby got in trouble.

Dad was a different type of manly father precisely
because he forgave us publicly for our transgressions and
didn't worry about their effect on his career; because he was
confident enough as a man to let Mom break the cultural
stereotypes of the time about how a mother and wife should
act; because he judged his success as a father by our happiness and not by any ego boost he'd attain from our achievements, or his own.

When my time came, I entered into manhood with
less clarity. I had that fixation that comes with being a

Kennedy—to be a great man on the big stage—and it would dictate most of my career moves for the next decade. But a good father would help me keep my ambitions in check until I could see, in my own life, the difference between greatness and goodness.

CHAPTER 12

◇

MAKING PEACE

After spending the second semester of my junior year in
London, I returned to Holy Cross for my senior year
and enrolled in a thesis program. My college adviser, John
Anderson, was also the mayor of Worcester and a big admirer
of Dad and the Kennedy and Johnson administrations. After
numerous conversations, I decided to write my thesis about
Lyndon Johnson, focusing on his early years as a poor son of
Texas, his first job as a teacher in Cotulla, Texas, and the
impact that experience had on his political ideology. I wanted
to better understand his life and the role my father had played
in creating and implementing so many of his ideals.

My college roommates often joked that my senior thesis
should be entitled "What My Daddy Did in the Sixties," but
the process was an eye-opener for me. I read voraciously
about Johnson's life and had many discussions with my dad
about him. Each time, Dad not only provided insights into
Johnson's thinking but also suggested top-level people with
whom I should speak.

When you are twenty-one years old and your father
recommends that you speak with a friend of his named Walter
Heller, you don't necessarily grasp the significance of who

this man is. I knew Mr. Heller had worked for Johnson, but I didn't understand the importance of the head of the President's Council of Economic Advisers, nor the significance of his resignation when Johnson refused to raise taxes after escalating the war in Vietnam. I simply thought of him as Dad's friend, an awfully nice man who was willing to spend an hour with me at National Airport before boarding a plane.

But it was the experience of writing about Johnson's life, his views on poverty, and his role in helping Dad create an independent Peace Corps that pushed me toward joining the Peace Corps myself. In the spring of my senior year, I applied. After waiting months to hear—no one from my generation had yet been accepted into the program—I learned that I would serve as an English teacher in Paraguay.

My roommates organized a going-away party for me in the fall of 1986 in Washington, D.C. We had a great weekend of fun and laughter, but I had begun to have concerns about leaving the country for nearly two and a half years. Twenty-seven months in a mud hut in the middle of Paraguay seemed like an eternity to a twenty-two-year-old. I thought I would be too far outside the action.

A few weeks before I was scheduled to go abroad, I went to see Dad. I knew how proud he was of the Peace Corps— barely a month earlier, in a huge tent on the National Mall, in front of thousands of people celebrating the twenty-fifth anniversary of the Peace Corps, Dad had given a terrific speech with a rousing finale. I'd been sitting in the front row, proud of him and motivated to serve, as he'd spoken:

> The Peace Corps seeks peace through service, not through
> economic strength or military power. Service is the heart
> and soul and substance of the Peace Corps. "Service" is a
> discredited word these days. Who wants to be a servant?
> No one! Service implies servitude, failure to achieve even

equality, let alone dominion. Yet the Peace Corps exists to serve, to help, to care for our fellow human beings. It works its magic from below, not from above. It concentrates on basics—food, health, education, community development. Peace Corps volunteers are rarely in capital cities, rarely seen with gilded potentates. They are almost un-American in their willingness to serve in the boondocks.

Peace Corps volunteers come home realizing that there are billions of human beings not enraptured by our pretensions, or practices, or morals . . . billions of human beings with whom we must live in peace. PCVs learn that there's more to life than money, more to life than the latest styles in clothes, cars, or cosmetics.

Suddenly I realize I do have a response to the original title given me for my speech. They asked me to talk about "the challenge of the Peace Corps." The challenge is simple to express, difficult to fulfill.

PCVs, stay as you are . . . be servants of peace . . . work at home as you have worked abroad, humbly, persistently, intelligently. Weep with those who are sorrowful, rejoice with those who are joyful.

Teach those who are ignorant. Care for those who are sick. Serve your wives . . . serve your husbands . . . serve your families . . . serve your neighbors . . . serve your cities . . . serve the poor. Join others who serve.

Serve, serve, serve! That's the challenge.

For in the end it will be the servants who save us all.

The place went crazy with applause. A few minutes after his speech, the emcee announced that I was going into the Peace Corps. He asked me to stand, and everyone clapped. I was the first of my generation to enroll in my father's creation.

Now, less than a month later, after a going-away party and that twenty-fifth-anniversary celebration, here I was, wavering about my decision to Dad, the man who'd founded the whole thing! I was scared; I felt like I was committing an act almost as shameful as Bobby's sixteen years before. But I should have known better; I should have known that the same love would come tumbling down on me.

Dad listened, never wincing or expressing disappointment, even with body language. He asked me what else I might be interested in doing. I told him that I wanted to serve in some capacity but I just couldn't fathom a two-and-a-half-year stint overseas. He didn't try to talk me out of my misgivings; he never mentioned that my decision to join the Peace Corps had been publicly announced just weeks ago. He never said how it made him feel—he never once used the word "I."

At the end of our conversation, he offered to connect me with people involved with VISTA (Volunteers in Service to America), the domestic version of the Peace Corps he'd started during President Johnson's administration. I eagerly agreed to go to the meeting. And as I toured VISTA's programs in rural Maryland, his words kept ringing in my ears:

"I support your decision not to go into the Peace Corps one hundred percent. Go see what you can learn about poverty right here in Maryland. If it interests you and you find a way to help the poor right here in our own backyard, maybe you can join that effort."

I was struck by how unconditionally supportive and understanding my father could be. But I still had that itch for politics—and the need to participate on the great stage as Kennedys were expected to.

◇

CHAPTER 13

MAKING A CHOICE

A few days after my VISTA tour, I was offered the opportunity to work as a special assistant for the newly elected governor of Maryland, William Donald Schaefer. I jumped at it. VISTA was an attractive option, but deep down, the world of politics held more allure for me. Schaefer had been the highly respected mayor of Baltimore, a man with a can-do approach to government. I had admired him from afar, and Dad thought that working for Schaefer, especially in the first few years of his administration, would open my eyes to all the issues affecting Maryland.

"This is a once-in-a-lifetime opportunity," Dad said. "You should take it—who knows what opportunities might arise for you to help Marylanders."

He was fully supportive of my career choice; actually, he was excited for me. I have always felt guilt pangs about turning down not one but two of his creations, but he never mentioned my demurrals again, focusing only on my well-being and progress.

I didn't quite know what the job entailed, but I couldn't wait to start. I was assigned to work for Schaefer's chief policy person, Alan Rifkin. Rifkin was a "whiz kid," the former chief of staff to the Senate president, Mickey Steinberg, who was now lieutenant governor.

I ended up as a glorified intern. I copied papers, answered the phone and letters from constituents, and got cups of coffee. I will never forget the first time I was called into Rifkin's office. I was thrilled; I didn't think he even knew I existed. When I walked into the room, Alan asked me to close the door. I did so, eager to hear what my assignment would be—finally, I was in! I was going to see how political deals were cut! Alan sat down behind his desk, pulled out a bag, handed it to me, and said, "These are my new license plates. My car is right out front. You can't miss it. Would you mind going down and changing my plates? Thanks a lot." Before I could say anything, he picked up the phone and started dialing.

I took the bag and headed to the parking lot in my new Jos. A. Bank suit, the one Dad had purchased for me a month earlier in celebration of my new job. I finished the task and, after the day was over, drove home to tell Dad what had happened.

I felt humiliated and confused, but Dad said, "Don't worry about it. Just keep working hard. Something good will happen. If you try hard and stay focused, it always does."

Shortly after the session was over, I received word that Governor Schaefer wanted me to work for him. The end result was that I was now a glorified intern for the governor, instead of for his chief policy adviser, but I was working for the governor and not lying on my back changing license plates.

During this time, I learned that Governor Schaefer was deinstitutionalizing the juvenile delinquent population in Maryland. Kids who, in the past, had been locked up for offenses as minor as skipping school were now being released back into the community, but they needed to be monitored.

So, too, did the more serious offenders need to be supervised. The problem was that Maryland had not developed community-based transition programs. I spent months researching effective programs so I could start such an effort in Maryland—the state needed those resources, and so did the kids.

After identifying the best model, which was operating in Massachusetts, I wrote a grant proposal to create a similar program in Maryland. I called it the Choice Program, in hopes that children would realize that they had choices in life, regardless of their situation. The grant proposal was turned down by a number of funders, but I secured two small grants, and the state government committed a small amount of money as well. I started the Choice Program in January 1988, working in Public School 180 in Baltimore.

The first year was tough—implementing any program from scratch is not easy. The "office" Arnett Brown, the principal of P.S. 180, gave me was actually a janitor's closet without a phone. Mr. Brown told me that I could work with the kids in his school who had been referred by the Juvenile Services Administration, but that was about the only thing he said to me. He was gruff and tough and had a booming voice you could hear anywhere in the school, a voice he used aggressively and often.

There was no air-conditioning in the building; that summer, I sweated through my shirt by eight o'clock every morning. The uniformly African American community was cut off by a highway, train tracks, and water on all sides. On my birthday, the entirely African American staff brought me a chocolate cake with chocolate icing—and one single white candle in the middle. That was me, they said, the lone white guy.

The program was simple: hire caseworkers who would see their charges three to five times a day, every day of the year.

They accomplished this feat by working in teams: a caseworker would meet with their own charges and their teammates' kids one night. The next morning, the team would debrief about what had happened overnight. Each caseworker would then see their kids that day and the night responsibility would rotate. The result was that a caseworker would work at least one night during the week and every fourth weekend. It was a demanding but rewarding job for the right person.

My first hire was not the right person for the job, despite the fact that I laid out the responsibilities clearly—or at least I thought I did. I didn't know what to do the first time I heard that James was not checking on his kids at night or on the weekend. The second time, I realized I needed to talk to him. James had played football, starting fullback no less. He was six feet tall and weighed well over two hundred pounds, most of which looked rock solid to me. When I asked him about his work and told him he had to check on the kids at night, he lifted me up by the throat and banged me against the school lockers. After he put me down and told me that he was quitting, I found myself shaking, with both fear and relief.

I got in my car, convinced that the program would never make it, that my start-up was bound to fail. What was I thinking—a young white kid working out of a closet in an African American school in an African American community? And the kids we were monitoring had been arrested for breaking the law; some of them already had been locked up, and some of them definitely were headed that way.

I had lost hope—I couldn't hire the right people; the caseworker job was too hard. I should just end it, I told myself, and give the funders back their money.

It took me forty-five minutes to drive from the poor Cherry Hill neighborhood of Baltimore to my parents' home in affluent northwest Washington. I opened the door, hopeless and embarrassed, nursing a sore neck and a desire to quit.

Dad turned down his beloved Bach on the stereo, and focused on me intently. He listened to the whole story and then said, "Don't worry about that guy. Go back and get to work. Those kids have been surrounded by people who have quit on them their whole lives. Don't be another person who just throws up their hands and leaves them. You are part of that school now, part of that community—go back there and work hard. You can make it happen."

It all sounded good, but I was still crushed. In my mind, clearly I had bitten off more than I could chew.

I said to Dad, "I hope I can make it happen. It's so hard. I can't believe it."

He looked at me as if I had spoken a foreign language. I don't think I ever heard him say, "I hope so." Not in his whole life. He went on about the kids as if he knew them directly, what they had suffered and all the people who had quit on them already. I realized later that Dad spoke to me that night from his own personal experience. He fought to end discriminatory practices in Chicago and had bricks thrown through his office window, yet he didn't lose hope and quit.

As head of Johnson's War on Poverty, he gave federal dollars directly to the poor, bypassing—in 1965—the state and local political structures. That's not the way it had been done in the past. Imagine giving federal dollars directly to poor African Americans in the segregated South so that they could create a Head Start program, a program that would give their kids a sound educational base to enter kindergarten ready to learn. And then he stood up and fought for that approach against powerful senators, congressmen, mayors, and even President Johnson. He didn't quit, and he won.

He also created the Legal Services program so that the poor would have access to lawyers. It seems so basic today, but in the mid-1960s, when he first proposed the idea and fought for it, it wasn't.

And he fought against President Reagan's efforts to downsize the Peace Corps, working with Loret Ruppe, the Reagan appointee who headed the Peace Corps. When he called Ruppe's office, he had to use a code name so that she would not get into trouble with the Reagan White House. Working with Dad meant working with the enemy to the Reagan White House, but Ruppe did, and together they ensured that the Peace Corps survived.

After dinner, I drove back to my apartment in Baltimore, energized to work my butt off. For the next three years, I earned $17,500 a year and put in six-plus days a week.

If I had known how much work a start-up involved, I probably would never have tried to do it. Convincing college graduates to drive around Baltimore day and night to monitor juvenile delinquents for $17,500 a year was a challenge. We paid them on time, but I had to scratch and claw for money. I accepted all contributions. Only once did I hesitate.

A friend introduced me to Father Bill Burke, a Catholic priest in Baltimore. Not only was Father Burke a warm, engaging man but he was also in charge of the Baltimore Catholic Campaign for Human Development. The campaign had money to give to organizations that helped the poor and the needy.

When I told Father Burke about my work, he smiled and said, "The campaign should support your efforts. Those kids need your help, and you need our help."

He sent me a check the next day. I was thrilled when I opened the envelope, but then I hesitated.

We were a secular nonprofit supported by private foundations and the state government. Should I accept money from the Catholic Church?

I called Dad and asked him.

"Hell, yes, take it," he said. "Those kids don't care if you're Catholic or Jewish or Muslim, do they? You took a check from my old friend Walter Sondheim, didn't you? Walter is Jewish. He cares about kids, and so does that priest.

"Those kids don't care what synagogue or church you go to—they only care that you are showing up every damn day. Take the check, deposit it, and then work with those kids."

It was one of our shortest phone calls ever.

A few months before Dad died, I came upon a speech he delivered in 1966 to the Xavier University Alumni Association. In it, he said:

> "Just three or four years ago, it was practically impossible for a federal agency to give a direct grant to a religious group. People said there was that wall between church and state. But we said that wall was put there to keep government out of the pulpit, not to keep the clergy away from the poor! That wall protects belief and even disbelief. It does not exclude compassion, poverty, suffering, injustice. That is common territory—not exclusively yours or mine but everybody's! With no wall between! And so we said, Reverend Mr. Jones, or Father Kelly, or Rabbi Hirsh, if you're not afraid to be seen in our company, we're not afraid to be seen in yours—because we are all about Our Father's business.

No wonder that call was so short—he had dealt with the issue some twenty-five years earlier.

Three years into its existence, an independent evaluation showed that the Choice Program reduced recidivism rates among its charges. George F. Will visited and wrote a glowing article in the *Washington Post,* noting,

> Choice is a low-budget, high-energy, labor-intensive, cost-effective program run by young adults willing to spend a year or more supervising troubled youths in this city's most troubled neighborhoods. The staff, divided into teams, is on call 24 hours a day, logging 200 miles a week in the wheezing cars they use to track and contact—three to five times a day, 365 days a year—the children assigned to them by public agencies.

In the fall of 1990, the program was going well, Mom and Dad were healthy, and though I was living in a two-bedroom apartment in Baltimore, I often visited them on the weekends. I was enjoying a more mature relationship with Dad, relying on him for practical support and advice. And on the weekends when I visited, my daily missives were slipped under my bedroom door. One Monday morning, I awoke to see two index cards and, just outside the door, a box. The first note read:

> Dear Mark—
> I needed to get an early start so I shoved off to catch 7:00 a.m. Mass downtown. Sorry to miss you. . . . But especially thankful to you am I. Why? For a super weekend of exercise, work, fun, and decisions. . . . Remember your mother will be home at dinner time tonight, 7:30–8:00.
> Love,
> Daddy

The second note was on top of the box.

Dear Mark,

I have gotten so fat I can't squeeze into these pants.

Maybe one of the boys in "Choice" would like to have them.

Love,

Dad

He knew that I was headed back to Baltimore for a week of work, but he still invited me home for dinner. And of course he wasn't too fat for his pants—he just wanted to give them away.

Things were going well enough that I took a weekend off and headed up to Holy Cross for a homecoming football game. At a tailgate party on a sunny, cool New England fall weekend, I was reintroduced to Jeanne Ripp. We had met a couple of times in college—Jeanne was a year behind me—but we didn't really know each other. We hit it off that Saturday afternoon; the next day, she had a ticket to a Red Sox play-off game, and so did I. I sat with Timmy and Dad at the game, down near Pesky's Pole. During the fifth inning, I went over to visit Jeanne and asked her to come over and meet Dad and Timmy during the seventh-inning stretch.

The Sox lost, but by the end of that weekend, I knew I had met my partner for life.

Life had gotten even better—I had a wonderful girlfriend, and the Choice Program won me some of the acclaim I craved on the "Kennedy Family Update Channel." But I felt I had to do more. That ridiculous bean counter in my brain was kachinging each sibling's and cousin's achievements and ranking mine alongside them. I had spent a good chunk of time in Annapolis, begging for money for the Choice Program. I had come to know a couple of the legislative leaders—Senator Frank Kelly, who chaired the Senate Budget and Taxation Committee, which not only dealt with the tax code but also approved the state budget, and Chairman Charles "Buzzy" Ryan and Tim Maloney, the two men who ran the House Appropriations Committee. Between the three of them—all Irish Catholics—they pretty much decided the Maryland state budget every year.

It became clear to me that I could head up a great program for troubled kids for the rest of my life and help thousands of kids yearly, or I could run for office and have an impact on the state budget and get into a position to help millions of kids. I also knew that politics was the way to keep up—rise, rise, rise, like a Kennedy should. My older cousin Joe Kennedy was already a congressman from Massachusetts; my older cousin Chris Kennedy was a high-level executive at the Merchandise Mart; my younger cousin Patrick Kennedy was a state representative in Rhode Island; Maria was a coanchor on NBC's Sunday *Today* show and had her own show called *First Person with Maria Shriver;* Anthony had founded the acclaimed program Best Buddies International. How was I going to compete with them without running for office?

This picture was in Dad's bedroom. Dad's godfather, Cardinal Gibbons, seated left, and President Howard Taft, seated right, visited Dad's childhood home in Westminster, Maryland. His father, Robert Sargent Shriver, Sr. is in the back on the far left. (BACHRACH PHOTOGRAPHY)

The Shriver Family Homestead in Westminster, Maryland. The grist mill is part of the building on the left. (RICHARD STACKS/*Baltimore Sun*)

Dad, upper left, with his brother, Herbert, and his parents, Hilda and Robert Sargent Shriver, Sr. on a trip to Atlantic City, New Jersey. (SHRIVER FAMILY COLLECTION)

Dad on June 18, 1922, the date of his First Communion, with the pastor of his church. Seventy-five years later, he added the following inscription on the back, just below where his mother had written a description of the day: "The information above was written by my Mother, Hilda Shriver, who with my Dad, Robert Sargent Shriver, gave me a happy, holy, & even joyful & long beginning to my life here on earth." (SHRIVER FAMILY COLLECTION)

Dad was captain of the baseball team at Canterbury. He's the only guy in the picture smiling! (R. SARGENT SHRIVER COLLECTION/JOHN F. KENNEDY PRESIDENTIAL LIBRARY)

Dad and his older brother, Herbert, left, in their Navy dress uniforms. (BACHRACH PHOTOGRAPHY)

Mom and Dad dated for seven years—but it was love at first sight for Dad! (R. SARGENT SHRIVER COLLECTION/JOHN F. KENNEDY PRESIDENTIAL LIBRARY)

Mom and Dad on their wedding day, May 23, 1953. They were married at St. Patrick's Cathedral in New York City by Cardinal Spellman. (SHRIVER FAMILY COLLECTION)

Dad and Dr. King's relationship began in Chicago in the 1950s. They are pictured here in the mid-1960s. (BETTMANN/ CORBIS/AP IMAGES)

With Senator Hubert Humphrey (second from right), Uncle Jack hands Dad the pen after signing the law creating the Peace Corps on September 22, 1961. (ABBIE ROWE/ JOHN F. KENNEDY PRESIDENTIAL LIBRARY)

As Peace Corps director, Dad traveled the world. Here he is washing his face in Tehran during a visit to Iran in 1964. (PEACE CORPS)

Jackie asked Dad to take responsibility for planning Jack's funeral. (ABBIE ROWE/ JOHN F. KENNEDY PRESIDENTIAL LIBRARY)

Dad headed the Office of Economic Opportunity (OEO) under President Johnson, while also serving as director of the Peace Corps. The book he's holding is entitled *Head Start*, a primer on one of the programs created under OEO. (SHRIVER FAMILY COLLECTION)

Dad in Harlem, speaking with local kids at a site that was being developed into a playground. (PAUL CONKLIN/TIME LIFE PICTURES/ GETTY IMAGES)

Dad hands out cigars at a cabinet meeting in the White House on February 18, 1964, the day after I was born. (PAUL SCHMICK)

Here I am at five days old in Mom's arms, as we prepare to leave Georgetown University Hospital. From left: Bobby, nine; Mom; Maria, eight; Timmy, four; and Dad. (HENRY BURROUGHS/ASSOCIATED PRESS)

Dad with his favorite son, me! (SHRIVER FAMILY COLLECTION)

A family portrait at Grandma Kennedy's house in Palm Beach. (SHRIVER FAMILY COLLECTION)

Mom and Dad rented Timberlawn, a two-hundred-acre farm in the Maryland countryside, when they moved to Washington, D.C., to join the Kennedy administration. (STACY RHODES)

We played all sorts of games at Timberlawn, including touch football. Here, Mom is dodging Bobby—just two months after giving birth to Anthony! (VIC CASAMENTO/ASSOCIATED PRESS)

Dad was sworn in as ambassador to France on May 7, 1968. He had a good relationship with French president Charles de Gaulle. (SHRIVER FAMILY COLLECTION)

Mom turned the American Embassy in Paris into a training facility for people with developmental disabilities. That's Timmy pushing a tire, which was part of an obstacle course inside the embassy. (PARIS MATCH)

A bicycle outing in Paris with Dad, left; me; Maria; our cousin, Sydney Lawford; Anthony in a hilarious outfit, and Mom. (SHRIVER FAMILY COLLECTION)

Richard "Rags" Ragsdale in Paris with Anthony in his left arm and me in his right, Timmy and Maria and an unidentified friend. (SHRIVER FAMILY COLLECTION)

◇

CHAPTER 14

ELECTION

After dating for a year, Jeanne and I were engaged in the fall of 1991 and married the following June. Jeanne had been living in Boston near her three brothers. I loved the area, and I had always wanted to get a master's degree, so I applied to Harvard and to Brandeis. I got into both schools and struggled with the decision; while I liked Brandeis a lot, Harvard was Harvard. But I had applied to the Kennedy School at Harvard and, frankly, I just wanted to escape the whole Kennedy thing for a while—to enjoy my new wife, learn, and meet new classmates with no labels attached.

Dad set things straight for me, though, when he said, "You need Harvard a lot more than Harvard needs you. Don't worry about what others are going to say about you. They'll always find something to complain about. Go to Harvard and learn as much as you can."

After my year at Harvard, Jeanne and I relocated to Maryland. We didn't have a home, so we moved in with my mom and dad. I often hear my friends say what a pleasure it is to relate to their parents as peers. We did this in an even more intimate way—under the same roof! For the few months we lived together, Dad never stopped prodding us to be more joyful.

One morning, I awoke to find a note under our door:

Dear Mark:
I notice you continue to cut your face quite often while
shaving.
   Believe me: if you will use this razor, almost any
shaving cream, this aftershave lotion, and this styptic
pencil in case you do cut your face, you will be able to
dispense with all the "toilet paper" applications. And
your face, and probably your wife, will thank you. You
will look and smell better!
Love, Daddy

I read it and laughed out loud—he noticed everything!
Here I was, a newlywed living with my parents, searching
for a house, and taking myself pretty seriously. And here was
Dad, poking some fun at me, yet caring for me at the same
time, and about even the smallest details in my life.

It was while living with my parents that I decided to run
for the Maryland House of Delegates. I took an unpaid leave
of absence from running the Choice Program, announced
my candidacy, and started campaigning immediately.

A core group of friends and I gathered every Tuesday at
seven-thirty A.M. at my parents' dining room table to discuss
the week's upcoming activities: fund-raisers, field operations, press relations, staffing, and so on.

My parents would sit at either end of the table and participate in the conversation. Mom pushed doing "tea parties,"
even getting Stephen Neill, my campaign manager, on the
phone with Polly Fitzgerald, who'd organized such parties
for Uncle Jack when he first ran for Congress, in 1946. Dad's
positive energy and joy never waned. My campaign chair,
Jonathan Weinberg, who led those meetings, encountered

Dad's famous—or infamous—impatience at one of our sessions.

"You were at a newspaper interview and this meeting was a particularly long one during which we strayed off topic too much for your father's liking. We just couldn't end it. It was eight forty-five, then nine o'clock, then nine-thirty. No one noticed that your Dad had gotten up and left.

"At about ten o'clock, he walked in with a bunch of yard signs under his arm and a list of doors to knock on. He coughed loudly and said, 'I don't know what all the geniuses are going to do, but I'm going to go to work and make a difference!' He turned around and walked out of the room." The message was clear: talk is necessary but so too is action.

Of course, the campaign got more complicated—a few months after I declared, my cousin Kathleen Kennedy Townsend was asked by Parris Glendening to join his ticket in the governor's race. *Here we go again,* I thought—I was trying to break out on my own but, once more, I was surrounded by the family. Ironically, Jeanne and I had chosen not to settle in Boston because so many cousins lived there; now, in Maryland, Dad's family's home for over two hundred years, I had a Kennedy cousin running in the same election cycle!

But two of us running at the same time didn't affect the primary results. By the time Jeanne and I arrived at the election night party at a local restaurant, it was clear that I was going to win. I had seen victory celebrations on television, but this was the first I had experienced in person. After all, Dad had come up short in 1972 and 1976, as had Uncle Teddy in 1980.

Mom and Dad were there, but since this was just the primary, my siblings had not come to town. (Kathleen won as well.) They were waiting for the general election. I spoke with each of them that night before giving my thank-you speech.

After Dad died, I received a letter from my friend Phil Lee, who'd been a member of the Tuesday morning breakfast club. Phil wrote:

> I will never forget the primary night election. Your father was so excited and happy. You were on the phone and I was in charge of press that night. A local television reporter needed to speak with you immediately. I ran over to tell you that you needed to get off the phone but your dad said no. I waited until he looked the other way, grabbed you, took your cell phone and hung up the call. Nothing was more important than press that evening. Or so I thought.
>
> Your father found me a couple of minutes later and yelled at me like I had never been yelled at before. He was so nice throughout the campaign, especially during those breakfast meetings, but this was a side of him I had never seen. I was stunned.
>
> Fifteen minutes later, the reason was clear. Someone told me that you were on the phone with your brother Bobby, and nothing was more important to Sargent Shriver than family. Not even press. I got the message loud and clear. And he was right.

Often, when politicians win, I've seen an excitement in their eyes that strikes me as unreal. Perhaps it is because at that moment, they think that everybody loves them. But in most cases, the supporters love the rush; they love that their futures might rise with yours. Few really love you. That night, however, and the night of my general election victory a few months later, Dad loved me no more or no less than before.

◇

CHAPTER 15

BREAK YOUR MIRRORS

I can't count the number of times someone has come up to me at an event or on a street corner or at an airport—in D.C., Chicago, Los Angeles, Miami, or anywhere, really—and said they had been so moved by something Dad had said in one of his speeches that they got up and did something about it. That was the common theme of his speeches over the years: Get up and do something about it! And so many people did act—whether it was fighting poverty, racial injustice, or the use of nuclear weapons or getting involved in Special Olympics.

It was funny that so many people remembered his speeches, because he wasn't as charismatic as President Kennedy on the stump, or Martin Luther King Jr. or Presidents Reagan or Clinton. You had to bear with him; his speeches were typically a crescendoing entirety, not barn burners full of memorable one-liners.

In 1994, he was invited to give the Class Day address at Yale. I was excited to go to New Haven to watch him, but also nervous. I had noticed a few slips and a little forgetfulness here and there. He was, after all, seventy-eight years old at the time—I wouldn't realize how bad things were for a few years still. But I had a strong sense that I had to attend this speech because, well, you reach a point in your parents' lives when you are never quite sure whether the next great moment will be the last great moment.

It was May 22, one day before Mom and Dad's forty-first wedding anniversary. Dad was a proud and accomplished Yale alum, and giving the Class Day address at any age, let alone at the age of seventy-eight, was a tremendous honor. As I watched him that sunny morning, I saw a focus and intensity that Dad usually hid behind his gregarious smile. This time he wasn't hiding it. He was treating this event like game day.

We applauded as he was introduced. He immediately mentioned Jackie, who had died just three days earlier. "There is no better time," he said,

> than this very moment to ask everyone here to remember a famous woman. I speak of Jacqueline Bouvier Kennedy Onassis. May the Yale class of 1994, and all the world, remember Jackie with respect and even pride. May they face death, when it comes, with integrity and composure and trust in God just as she did three days ago. May the loving God give her peace and joy in heaven for all eternity.

After all of us observed a moment of silence in her honor, Dad made fun of himself:

> Despite these sudden, serious, and personal comments, many of you may not know much about me—not my past or my work, or my plans for the future.
>
>   Nevertheless, I am a man of consequence—the Sargent Shriver known everywhere as Maria Shriver's father!
>
> But I've never sought the spotlight. I always wanted

to be private, remain in the background, be rather anony-
mous. That's why in 1972 I ran with George McGovern.

All of you are too young to remember that campaign, but it was the first time when the faces of the
Democratic candidates were found on milk cartons, like
those of missing children. Ironically, our opponents about
three years later became "missing children" themselves.

Fortunately, I have always felt completely at home
here at Yale and on the old campus. The moment I first
arrived in New Haven, I settled down in the luxury of 201
Wright. I can hardly believe it, but that was sixty years
ago. But some things never change. When I graduated, all
of us seniors felt exactly as you feel now: we hoped and
prayed the graduation speaker would be brief—if possible,
very brief! So I'll be exactly that today.

I've chosen a simple but rather unusual message for
you. It's just this: I wish I were you!

Right off the bat, he blew me, and the audience, away
with that line: "I wish I were you!"

And then he followed it up with this: "Not because I
wish I were young again, but because for the first time in five
hundred years, the new century, the twenty-first century,
can be the first without cataclysmic war."

He was calling on the graduating class—all of us,
really—to be warriors for peace.

Then he again said, "I wish I were you!"

And then a third and a fourth time, all booming.

He used this line as the speech's refrain. *What a smart
way to identify with the audience,* I thought. And by all the
nodding heads, I could tell that Dad had connected with
these kids. He went on to challenge the graduates to work
together to redefine the world, no small task indeed. But he
wasn't done. He quoted Martin Luther King Jr.:

"You ought to believe in something in life, believe that thing so fervently that you will stand up with it till the end of your days."

Then he said, "Now then, young men and women, in what will you believe?" And he laid out the challenge to believe in peace:

> Leaving Yale today, each of you is called on to be a peacemaker. No calling is higher, no calling is more needed. You are called on to be peacemakers in your families. In your neighborhood and your workplaces. If you want to eliminate weapons from the world, first we must get them out of our own hearts.

Peace, to Dad, meant more than just the absence of war—it meant hard work to sustain peace among nations, and it also meant hard work to sustain peace in ourselves, in our families, in our communities, and in our country. He challenged those graduates to do that work by joining the Peace Corps, by working for the Job Corps, or by volunteering for Special Olympics.

And then he said that even though he had been "blessed" by the opportunity to participate in some of the great peacebuilding endeavors of the twentieth century, his "greatest happiness has been my wife and five children. . . . None of them came to me as a result of my brains, my hard work, or my education. . . . They really came to me from God. I say from God because that's the complete truth! To a political or solely secular audience, I'd say they came to me as a result of 'good luck.' But, truthfully, it hasn't been luck. It's been 'love.' God's love is something no one earns. It's just given."

At Yale! Mentioning God so profoundly at fully secular, powerful Yale! *Wow,* I thought, *what's next?* Dad warned the graduates that the task of making peace, of moving it "away from the side show to the center stage," was going to be a challenge:

> And I have one small word of advice, because it is going to be tough: Break your mirrors! Yes, indeed—shatter the glass. In our society, which is so self-absorbed, begin to look less at yourself and more at each other. Learn more about the face of your neighbor and less about your own.
>
> I suggest this: When you get to be thirty, forty, fifty, or even seventy years old, you'll get more happiness and contentment out of counting your friends than counting your dollars. You'll get more satisfaction from having improved your neighborhood, your town, your state, your country, and your fellow human beings than you'll ever get from your muscles, your figure, your automobile, your house, or your credit rating.
>
> You'll get more from being a peacemaker than a warrior. I've been both, so I speak from experience. Break the mirrors!
>
> Be peacemakers of the community and you and your family will be happy!

This advice, which he shouted out again and again with a voice mixing exhortation and outrage, shook me. I bet it left those students and their parents moved and motivated, but it rattled me. I already had a sense of this being his last hurrah, but now I felt like he was speaking directly to me. He'd cut to the core of the question that had most bugged me during my adolescence and adult life: how not to be led astray by cultural or family expectations, how to avoid the traps of perceived but misguided greatness?

When Dad finished, the applause was tremendous. As the larger ceremony wrapped up, I couldn't stop thinking about his words. And then the image of Jesus raising hell in the temple popped into my head. As a kid, one of my favorite Bible scenes was of an outraged Jesus ransacking the corrupt temple because of the sinful practices he'd witnessed there. I loved the rebel impulse, the rage, the disdain for materialism that simply erupted in him.

Dad's exhortation for us to shatter mirrors reminded me of this passage. Dad was a radical, a hell-raiser who based his revolutionary public service on very orthodox instruction manuals: the Scriptures, his faith's creeds and prayers, and the life of Jesus Christ. You may have heard the phrase "applied mathematics." I don't know what the hell it means. But I know that Dad lived out applied religion. He applied his faith's ethics every day to everything he did. His paradox—his radical orthodoxy—allowed him to conform to the requirements of a life in public service while blowing up politics from the inside, like he did when he convinced Jack to call Coretta Scott King or when he created the Peace Corps.

I just watched him that day, just drank him in. Some sons are driven to try to be as great as, or even greater than, their fathers. I didn't give a hoot about that; I knew I never would be. But that afternoon I understood that I had to start to try to be as good as he was, as decent and generous and joyful as he was. I didn't know it then, but that aspiration to goodness rather than greatness made for even harder work.

The achievement of greatness in America is easily measured: money in the bank, job titles, press coverage, appearances on TV. The more difficult challenge of living a life defiantly and incessantly devoted to faith, hope, love, and family was the taller order—as well as doing it without the applause and recognition.

My favorite example of Dad's steadfast goodness had happened a few years earlier, when we opened the new Choice Program office in Baltimore. Actually, all we'd gotten was a bunch of portable trailers slapped together on top of a deserted basketball court, but it was a new office, and Governor Schaefer came to the grand opening on a wet and dreary Saturday morning. Everyone was joyful and busy, as community members helped Choice staff plant trees and shrubs all around the perimeter. The press was there, and so, too, were my parents.

When Schaefer arrived, everyone beelined over to him, myself included.

I was so focused on Schaefer that I didn't notice Dad. But soon I turned around and caught a glimpse of him off to the side, chatting earnestly with an eight- or nine-year-old African American boy. It was an animated discussion—both were gesticulating and laughing, and it must have lasted a good five minutes. Dad had the utmost respect for Schaefer, but he never budged from his conversation with that kid. He was in the moment; the kid was the only human being in Dad's line of vision. For now, everyone else, including the governor and me, could wait.

Even then I knew that Dad's uniqueness lay in moments like this, in his insistence on the grandeur of all the relationships in this sticky human web that connects all of us.

But I succumbed too often to the trappings of my generation's culture. We race around, consumed with transitory things like what we wear and who we know, the shape of our bodies, our kids' athletic accomplishments, our school's rankings, our cars, our office size and its location, because we can afford to and because we think we have to. Most of us never walked through the fire like Dad's generation did, and therefore didn't emerge valuing the simplicity and importance of life's essentials like faith and hope and love. Those ideals remain words in the Bible instead of stamps on the brain because the rat race dismisses them as antiquated, impractical, or even self-defeating.

I grew up with faith, hope, and love as explicit topics in

my household and with a father who embodied and lived by these three tenets—on the world's stage and in our living room. As I matured, I grew to understand how Dad's devotion to three single-syllable words drove his life and work. But I never fought in a war like Dad did; I never lived through the Great Depression like he did; I never experienced the devastating violence that his generation of our family did; I never really put everything on the line for civil rights, racial justice, and social progress like he did.

And, for this reason, I think I had an emotional but not a foundational stake in them. I liked to think about faith, hope, and love at church and talk about these ideas with my kids. But apart from a few minor struggles, I never needed them as if life depended on them.

My pillars were made of reinforced concrete—strong enough, largely thanks to my father and his lessons. But his were made of steel, or titanium, or whatever the hardest metal is.

It is ironic that so often the first time we have to use them for real—our parents' principles and examples and tools—comes when they themselves age, suffer, and die. My capacity for faith, hope, and love wasn't truly battle-tested like his—until the day we learned what he would die from, and the ways in which he was going to suffer in the years leading up to his death.

PART II

PART II

◇

CHAPTER 16

THE THIRD BASEMAN

One of the great pleasures of my childhood was driving up I-95 with Dad to Baltimore to watch Orioles baseball games. He would talk about the goings-on in Washington and tell us stories about being the captain of his high school team and playing at Yale. He loved playing catcher because it put him in the middle of the action, calling pitches and moving fielders around to take advantage of the batter and the pitch count. At Yale, he often recalled, his team had faced the Washington Senators during an exhibition game.

He would also tell us about sneaking in to watch the then–minor league Baltimore Orioles play when he was a young boy. They played in an old wooden stadium built in 1914, located on what is today Twenty-ninth Street and Greenmount Avenue. It burned down in 1944. Dad would reminisce about watching the great minor leaguers, such as Lefty Grove, who would go on to a Hall of Fame career in the major leagues.

I knew the Orioles only as a major league team, one that played in the northern section of Baltimore, on Thirty-third Street. We would get off I-95 and head toward the Inner

Harbor, and Dad would start pointing out all the important parts of the city.

"The Inner Harbor! A number of years ago, it was all decrepit, decaying buildings, and so much of it was burned out after the riots in the 1960s. Mayor Schaefer has done a wonderful job rebuilding this area, attracting business and creating jobs. He has to focus on the school system now, but he's done a great job downtown."

He'd take a left and head up Charles Street. "The Washington Monument. Everyone in Washington, D.C., thinks the Washington Monument in that city is the first one built in honor of George Washington. But that one in front of us? That's the first one in the country.

"And over to your left, that's the first cathedral in America. I went to the Cathedral School, right next door, and I was an altar boy at the cathedral itself. Does anyone know who designed it?"

Before we could answer, he'd blurt out, "Henry Latrobe, the same man who designed the U.S. Capitol. That's where my godfather, Cardinal Gibbons, used to live, and right around the corner is where my mom and dad worked feeding the poor in Baltimore."

Inevitably, another driver would swerve in front of him.

"Good God," he'd scream, "that fool just cut me off!" But he'd never be distracted for long.

"Up the road a bit is the great Johns Hopkins University, one of the best universities in all the country," he'd tell us. "I used to play lacrosse on the Hopkins field. We were called the Hopkins Midgets. But I am not going to stay on Charles Street all the way up to Thirty-third. If we take a right on Thirty-third, the traffic will be terrible. Let's cut down here to the right." He'd jerk the car to the right and off we'd go, cutting through alleys and side streets until the final turn that dropped us one block from the stadium.

"Hurry up," he'd yell, pulling the car into a spot out front. "Palmer is pitching, and he's going to win the Cy Young Award this year." He'd slam down the parking brake and yell again: "Let's go!" And out of the car we'd tumble, running to the stadium with Dad right alongside us.

I watched an aging Brooks Robinson play against the Red Sox in 1977, fumbling a ground ball at third base. When he retired, a few months later, Dad was crushed. I was nervous when a rookie first baseman started getting a lot of time on the field in 1977. Could we win the division, battling the hated Yankees and Red Sox, with this rookie playing so much? No, but Eddie Murray performed spectacularly, even though we ended up losing to the Yankees by two and a half games. In the 1979 World Series, when we went up three games to one against the Pittsburgh Pirates, I bet my cousin Chris Kennedy that the Orioles were going to win. I remember thinking him such a fool for taking the bet. Paying him off after the Orioles squandered the lead hurt almost as much as the loss of the series itself.

We four brothers and Dad even went on a road trip to Toronto at the end of the 1989 pennant race, only to see the Orioles lose on Friday and Saturday and be eliminated from the play-off chase. We traveled to New York to watch the Orioles sweep the Yankees late in the 1983 season. We had to be escorted out of Yankee Stadium by the police after fans threw liquor bottles at us.

At the end of a game, Dad would often walk us down to the locker room and introduce himself to the attendant out front, who'd let us in. It was both thrilling and embarrassing to step into a locker room of twenty-five naked men, all of whom you idolized. But that didn't stop Dad. He'd head right in and start shaking hands, with a big smile on his face. He became good friends with Mark Belanger, the great shortstop; Rick Dempsey, the legendary Baltimore catcher; Mike

Flanagan, the left-handed pitcher from New Hampshire who won the Cy Young Award in 1979 and whose father worked for Dad in the New Hampshire primary in 1976; and Doug DeCinces, the Orioles' third baseman who'd replaced Brooks Robinson. He would seek them out and introduce us to them. They'd talk about the game, and DeCinces and Flanagan in particular loved to hear Dad's Washington stories, too.

I was destined to become a baseball junkie. We lived out the classic father-son dynamic only baseball fosters. He used to hit us kids fly balls in the backyard; we played a fielding game called pepper and tossed a baseball around almost every summer night when we weren't at the ballpark. During the summer of 1981, I watched him hit fly balls to Dwight Evans and Carl Yastrzemski—Major League Baseball was on strike that summer, and the two Boston Red Sox greats were working out with the Harwich Mariners baseball team of the Cape Cod League. He also hit ground balls to the Harwich Mariners' shortstop until the guy almost fell over. The shortstop was a sophomore in college; Dad was sixty-six years old.

Arriving at Memorial Stadium one hot July day in 1990 was like subjecting ourselves to voluntary suffocation. The Baltimore blacktop seethed; a cloud of humidity and cigarette smoke hovered over the stadium; even my ears were sweating as we sat beside the field; and when I stood up to go get a hot dog, I felt like my feet were sloshing in my sneakers.

But, oh, how lovely it was! Dad loved baseball, he loved Baltimore, and he loved the ritual of fathers and sons and the American game. Even as a boy, I was aware of the transformation that would come over him as we walked down the steps at the ballpark. His face lit up, his step quickened, his eyes fixated on the field. During the game he sat mesmerized, diligently analyzing each pitch and play, looking down only to memorialize an out or a hit on his scorecard.

On that hot day in Baltimore, I was twenty-six. But I still felt like a kid, and I could tell Dad did, too—even though in fact he was an aging man and I a newly arriving man.

We sat behind the first base dugout, and above us, in section 34, a guy named Wild Bill Hagy led beer-drenched chants of O-R-I-O-L-E-S! A Baltimore cab driver, he contorted his beer belly and long beard and cowboy hat into the shape of each letter.

Dad loved the whole spectacle, from Wild Bill to John Denver's "Thank God I'm a Country Boy" during the seventh-inning stretch. I always felt like he was more at home here than with the hotshots in D.C. It wasn't that he disliked celebrity and power; he just wasn't consumed by it. He engaged with an athlete in Special Olympics with the same attentiveness and devotion as he did with Paul Newman.

But ballplayers were his exception. Dad used to talk about some of the minor league players he grew up watching as if they were Babe Ruth. He remembered plays and players and spoke about them with a vividness and enthusiasm that I inherited.

That day, when the Orioles' third baseman made a leaping stab on a sharp grounder over the bag, steadied himself on one knee, and threw a bullet straight across the diamond to beat the runner by an inch, Dad jumped up and lifted his fists. I did, too.

As he sat down, he shouted, "Just like Belanger used to do it!"

A few people around us chuckled.

Then he said it again.

"You mean Brooks, Dad," I said. "Brooks Robinson!"

He looked at me with a scorn that my polite correction did not merit.

"What are you talking about?" he asked. "Anyone knows Belanger was the greatest third baseman of his generation!"

I let it go. But inside I couldn't forget it. What the hell was he talking about? This man so precise of mind and memory was terribly confused. Belanger a third baseman? Brooks Robinson—you have got to be joking, Dad. You *are* joking, right?

I blamed it on the Baltimore heat. He was seventy-five. The temperature didn't seem to have dropped a degree after the sun went down. The night grew even more humid. Yes, the heat was to blame, I told myself, and I got up and went to get a beer.

◇

CAR CRASH

The next time, there was no heat to blame.

A few months after that game, Mother was in a car crash on Canal Road in Washington, D.C., that left her crushed behind the wheel of her vehicle.

The paramedics extracted her with the Jaws of Life— they literally cut her out of the car to put her on a stretcher so that they could transport her to the emergency room.

I rushed to the hospital and into the back of the ER. There was Mom laid out on a table, machines all around her, and Dad standing beside her. He stared blankly and could barely speak. He was in shock, I think, watching the love of his life and his wife of thirty-seven years lie there at the edge of death.

At my first glimpse of Mom, mangled and heaving on the bed, I'd gasped. But I'd quickly recovered. I'd known it would be bad—Rags had called me and prepared me for the sight. Once I saw her chest moving up and down, I knew she would live. She was as thin as a rail and had suffered broken bones and countless other ailments in the past, but she always bounced back quickly and, it seemed, even stronger than before. She was a force of nature, and a relentless one, too. Her body was beaten up, but I knew that her spirit was strong. She was too young to die, I thought, and she had willed herself through so much in the past. I felt, I just knew, that she would will herself through this one, too.

But I wasn't ready to behold Dad. Physically, he looked okay—there was no blood, no bruises; he hadn't been in the car. But he was a ghost of himself, more ghostly than even Mom. She had been in a terrible car crash; he was watching his love and his life crash right in front of him. Dad was always the man who summoned grace under pressure. I had never seen him wobble or quake. His faith had sustained him through hardships and travails worse than I could have even imagined. But here his love was being threatened, and that shook him like nothing I had ever seen.

◇

My instinct that day in the ER was right. Mom survived and thrived; she was back at the Special Olympics office within a few months. But Dad—in conversations, at meals, during cocktail hour—seemed to be lingering instead of animating those events in his usual manner. I don't think he ever fully recovered—or at least my view of him was altered by my having seen him in such a vulnerable state for the first time.

In 1992, Mom and Dad hosted an engagement party for Jeanne and me. We had invited about seventy-five people to their house in Maryland for cocktails and hors d'œuvres. It was a beautiful day, and I felt the sort of lightness and joy that I suppose Dad felt most days of his life.

Then Dad clinked his fork against his glass and announced that he wanted to make a toast. The room hushed; I felt a deep love come over me. I was proud, too. I was committing to an amazing woman but also to the same fidelity, devotion, and loyalty that Dad had lived out in his marriage with Mom. My father standing to toast Jeanne and me on this night felt like the final rite of passage into adulthood and gave me hope that I would replicate his success as a husband and father.

He welcomed everyone, cracked a few jokes, thanked my mother for hosting the event, and then started speaking about Jeanne and me.

It was a great toast, except that he kept referring to Jeanne as "that beautiful woman over there standing next to my son." My soon-to-be mother-in-law was in town for the party, and he referred to her a couple of times as "that beautiful woman's equally beautiful mother." He wrapped it up, and everyone applauded. I don't know whether anyone else noticed that both Jeanne's name and her mother's name had escaped Dad—I doubt it, because he was so engaging and eloquent—but it worried me.

I began to rationalize it as I moved about the room: if he could forget that Brooks Robinson—Brooks Robinson, of all people—had played third base for the Orioles, then I could surely forgive him for letting Jeanne's name slip. He was an old-timer now, I thought, and his memory should be lauded instead of condemned for the occasional slipup. But still I couldn't shake my concern, and I walked through the rest of the night with half my brain chatting with our guests and the other half reliving his toast.

He held it together on the big stages. He was traveling, giving speeches around the world. And he could still rock the house. Sure, he seemed to ramble a bit, to go off the subject occasionally, but he had an uncanny ability to tie all the loose pieces together and end with a crescendo, sending people away energized and motivated to rededicate their lives to peace, the elimination of poverty, and service of all sorts.

◇

CHAPTER 18

THE WANDERER

Dad devoured the campaign trail during those short-lived but enchanting days in 1972 and 1976 when he was running for vice president and then president.

He had a campaign manager, but Dad was unmanageable as a campaigner. He would get out there and start meeting people and the schedule would go out the window. He always seemed to forget that politicians campaign to win votes, not to make new friends all over the country. He made plenty of new friends, but he never got enough votes.

So it was no surprise to me that, when I ran for the Maryland House of Delegates in 1994, Dad, even at seventy-nine, hit the campaign trail with enthusiasm. Each morning he would show up at the office, grab a list of names and addresses, and head out to knock on doors and shake hands. Rags usually drove him, but occasionally Dad would venture out on his own, find the appointed street, park his car, grab his list, the campaign literature, and some yard signs, and start pounding the pavement.

He would come back at the end of a long day—six or seven hours in the summer heat in Washington would tire anyone, let alone an older man—always with a smile on his face and a kick in his step.

Then one day my campaign manager, Stephen Neill, called me aside. He looked concerned, and I readied myself for news of a poor poll. Instead he told me about Dad's day. He had paid a visit to a gentleman who worked at a local Jiffy Lube. The man, stunned to find Sargent Shriver on his doorstep, invited Dad in for a glass of iced tea. Dad, of course, accepted and then spent the better part of an hour talking to the man about his job. He told Stephen that the man would be willing to send a letter to his coworkers at Jiffy Lube on behalf of my candidacy. Dad also convinced the man to speak with someone from Special Olympics about the possibility of hiring people with developmental disabilities at all the Washington-area Jiffy Lube stores.

Then Stephen started laughing. "I think your father is losing it," he said. "He's out there for over six hours and spoke with just a handful of people. And how many votes are we going to get from Jiffy Lube? He's out of his mind!"

Part of me agreed with Stephen, but another part of me immediately started defending Dad. I assured Stephen that when Dad left that house, he had that guy's vote. He didn't knock on a lot of doors, but he sure made people feel important. And that was important, too. Driving home that night, though, I felt just as frustrated as I had at my engagement party. Why the hell was he acting this way?

◇

I won the election, and we all overlooked Dad's meanderings. I was happy for myself but almost as much for him—I wanted Dad to cherish the spectacle of his son serving in the same elected position as his own grandfather Thomas Herbert Shriver. I wanted these to be his glory days, for him to step back and smell those black-eyed Susans that, he always reminded me, were the state flower of Maryland.

But it was in that stately town of Annapolis that I finally

realized he had a terrible problem. Each spring, I would invite
constituents for a party and update them on the work I was
doing. In 1999, my fifth year in office, I invited the Speaker
of the House of Delegates, Casper Taylor, to say a few words.
"Cas" was from Cumberland, Maryland, not too far from
Union Mills, and had long admired Dad. They had met when
I was sworn in, and again many times during Dad's visits.
But this year, when Cas came over to talk to us, Dad struggled
to make the connection. After a few minutes of idle chitchat,
he turned to Cas and said, "What exactly do you do down
here in Annapolis? You seem like a talented fellow—what
role do you play?"

Cas took it in stride and explained that he was the
Speaker of the House, a fact I had told Dad often and then
again just a few minutes before the event.

The Brooks Robinson slipup came back to mind, and the
other moments of forgetfulness over the last few years suddenly added up. I had denied the gravity of each and every
incident. I had never allowed myself to think of his behavior
as a symptom of a disease. Dad was such a lion that I thought
he would keep living long and hard and then keel over one
day in some distant land—a death befitting a dashing life.

At the end of the night, as I said good-bye to him, a
wave of sadness buckled me at the knees. My father loved
Maryland politics and had always known all the players.
And here he was, the man with a Rolodex in his brain, not
recognizing the Speaker of the House!

As he got in the car and Rags nodded and drove off, I
just stood there. I shook my head and clenched my fists and
thought, *Why are you getting old just as I'm getting my political
career going? You are going to miss out on so many of the important
events of my life—my kids, my career—and I need your sage advice
and you can't give it to me.* I turned back to the statehouse and
felt at once angry, sad, and confused.

I wanted to say to him: Your faith was always so strong and convincing that it rubbed off on me, it carried me along, but now I am losing faith in you. And I don't know what to do.

A part of me blamed Dad. I wanted to ask, Don't you know you are breaking my heart?

◇

CHAPTER 19

BIRTHDAY PARTY

My wife, Jeanne, is the youngest of seven children—she has three older brothers and three older sisters—and I am the fourth of five. When we were dating seriously, we talked a couple of times about how many kids we would like to have if we ever got married. The number was at least five—maybe more if we were lucky! Jeanne's oldest sister had her first son, Gregor, when Jeanne was only nine years old, so she was always surrounded by lots of family members. And I grew up with twenty-eight first cousins on the Kennedy side and three on the Shriver side, so the vibe was always the more, the merrier.

There is an old saying, however, that if you want to give God a good laugh, tell God your plans. So it was on the childbirth front. We were hoping for baby after baby, but it was not meant to be. Just two months after Jeanne got pregnant for the first time, we suffered our first miscarriage. The second miscarriage came barely six months later. And then we heard the overwhelming news that three miscarriages before a first birth is a strong signal that you probably will not be able to have any children at all.

The pressure of getting elected was nothing like the pressure I felt about trying to have a baby. What's more,

Anthony and Alina, who got married a year after us, already had three; Timothy and Linda had four, and Linda was pregnant with their fifth. Maria had four children as well.

The time from 1995 to mid-1997 was dominated not by my budding political career or my new job at a telecommunications company called LCI but by our efforts to have a baby. Doctors' visits were much more important than bill hearings and stock prices. And I was the source of the pressure for Jeanne to get pregnant.

When everything failed and we—really, I—let go and understood that the doctors weren't miracle workers, that's when Jeanne got pregnant. We didn't tell anyone except our parents until Jeanne was well into her third month. It was the fall of 1997 and my 1998 reelection campaign for the House of Delegates was gearing up, but this race was not as close as the first, and my mind was focused almost exclusively on Jeanne and the pregnancy. It was such an exciting time. The kicking in Jeanne's stomach, the preparation of the baby's room, and the trips to the baby stores—we were flying in the clouds. All the sonograms indicated that the baby was healthy and small. We didn't know if it was going to be a boy or a girl; we wanted to get the news the old-fashioned way. On February 16, the day before my birthday, we went to the hospital convinced that the baby was coming, but after an hour or so, we were sent home. A false alarm. We waited another two weeks before the doctor told us that he wanted to induce on March 6.

That was another day when I felt the magic that Dad, I think, regularly felt in his life. I don't think my feet touched the ground the whole day. I drove Jeanne to Georgetown University Hospital, dropped her off, and then rushed to the airport to pick up her oldest sister, Susan, a labor and delivery nurse who had flown in from Buffalo to be by Jeanne's side. Susan and I beelined back to the hospital, and as I pulled in, Susan jumped out of the car and raced to the room. After I parked the car, I ran as fast as I could. And then we waited . . . and waited.

Our doctor believed in a slow approach, so the process that started at seven in the morning on March 6 was not over until twelve forty-six A.M. on March 7.

Our first visitors the next day were Mom and Dad. Even though Mary Elizabeth "Molly" Shriver was their twelfth grandchild, Mom and Dad were as excited as could be. Molly had a tiny bit of strawberry peach fuzz on her head and the bluest eyes. She weighed in at five pounds, twelve ounces. She was the most beautiful creature I had ever seen in my life.

Mom had an immediate connection with Molly and would come over to our house every day after work to visit her. She would walk in the front door even as she was knocking on it, and head to Molly's squeals. If Jeanne and I were in the room, she would say hi and then get on the floor and start playing with the baby. She would barely acknowledge us during the rest of her visit. From now on I would be second fiddle to Molly in Mom's eyes. But I loved watching Mom in her role as grandmother—dancing in the backyard or crawling around in the bushes with Molly alongside her, looking for leprechauns.

Just ten months later, we learned that Jeanne was pregnant again. This time, the due date was in late fall 1999. Once again, Susan joined us in the delivery room. Jeanne had a new doctor who believed in getting the baby out as quickly as possible. The induction started at seven-thirty A.M., and by eleven o'clock, Jeanne was in the final stages of childbirth. The doctor and Susan helped Jeanne through the process while I held her hand, muttered words of encouragement, and stayed out of the way.

But Dad didn't! You could hear him out in the hall pacing back and forth, talking. He was on the prowl. He had not been allowed into the room when Mom gave birth; Dad told us that in those days, you kissed your wife good-bye when you got to the hospital, and the next time you saw her was when a nurse wheeled her into her room. Mom's hair would be brushed and the baby swaddled in a warm blanket. It was a vision right out of a 1950s movie.

We didn't invite him into the birthing room either, but we could hear him outside our door, asking nurses and doctors—anyone—for updates. On his thirteenth grandchild!

And then, moments after our son Thomas Kennedy Shriver was born, Dad couldn't take it anymore. He burst into the room. He had slipped just a few months earlier in Annapolis, but nothing was holding him back today.

"Congratulations!" he shouted. "A baby boy! A wonderful nurse gave me the news. Wow! How are you feeling, Jeanne?" Before Jeanne could answer, he cried out, "Oh my goodness, there he is over there in the corner. He's beautiful!" He couldn't contain himself. He was gesticulating wildly, and I could see the rosary beads in his hands. I am pretty sure he had never been in a room with a two-minute-old baby in his life. The doctor didn't say a word. She was making sure that Jeanne was okay.

Dad kept talking: "What are you going to name him? My, what a big, handsome boy. He's beautiful, Jeanne, he really is. Wow!"

And then Timmy walked in. "I'm sorry to bust in, Jeanne," he said as he grabbed Dad. "He's been out here pacing and praying, but I couldn't hold him back. Come on, Dad, let's leave Jeanne alone for a few minutes." But Timmy lingered in the room, too.

Molly appeared about fifteen minutes later; I looked around and took in the scene. We were now a family of four, joined by a brother and a sister and Dad. Tommy wasn't an hour old, and he was already at his first family party!

And right in the middle of it was his eighty-four-year-old grandfather, laughing and chatting and praying.

◇

CHAPTER 20

UP IN FLAMES

In June 1999, I picked up the phone to hear Rags yelling, "Markie, get your ass over here fast! Your parents' house is on fire! Hurry up!"

I immediately jumped into my car and drove the three miles to their home, wondering how the fire had started, hoping that Mom and Dad hadn't caused it. I arrived to a chaotic scene straight out of the movies: fire trucks in the driveway, television camera crews outside the front gate, people everywhere. I ran up to a fireman, who assured me that the fire had been put out. Inside, the house was drenched with water, and there were holes in the wall around the dining room fireplace. Evidently, the fire had started in a wall in my mother's room, on the second floor, and the firefighters had used their axes to open the wall below her room in order to find out if the fire was still burning.

Mom and Dad were at the Special Olympics office. I was relieved and also embarrassed for having assumed they'd had a hand in the fiasco.

I spent an inordinate amount of time over the next year and a half helping my parents look for a rental home, working with them to rebuild their house, and managing the insurance claim. I sat with them as they sorted through what to throw away and what to keep, figuring out what had historical value and what was accumulated junk. I needed a new compartment in my brain to sustain all that was going on. But the most draining and time-consuming task was serving as the lead negotiator between Mom and Dad. Yes, they relied heavily on each other for advice and help, but they were also both strong-willed, independent people. While Mom focused on increasing the quality of each and every Special Olympics games, Dad wanted to expand Special Olympics all over the world. And so it was on the house front. Dad would decide to paint a room white and then leave on a trip; Mom would come home, tell the painters to make it light blue, and then head out for a Best Buddies fund-raiser. It was a logistical nightmare. I found myself irritated and frustrated but still exhilarated by their energy and intensity.

While Mom went to the office the day after the fire and continued working as if nothing had happened, Dad continually checked in with me for updates. With two kids of my own at home, I felt what so many adults in their thirties and forties feel: that between caring for our parents and raising our children, we are losing control. We are spread too thin to stay on top of so many things. My dad's mental decline devastated me; the crumbling house seemed the perfect symbol for their grand lives now full of fissures and gaps.

I felt a duty to take care of my parents as they had always taken care of me. So many people say you end up becoming a parent to your parents. That notion, for me, falls far short of the truth. A parent can pretty much control a five-year-old. I couldn't control anything, least of all two insistent and aging people.

◇

In late 2000, just a year and a half after the fire and while they were still rebuilding their home, Mom was diagnosed with a pancreatic tumor. The doctor recommended surgery to determine if the tumor was cancerous. As usual, Mom didn't hesitate; she made the decision for an immediate operation. I am sure she thought that the sooner she had the tumor out, the sooner she would be up and about. The surgery was a success; the tumor turned out to be benign, and Mom was discharged a few days later. But a few days later, she was headed back to Johns Hopkins Hospital with severe pain in her side.

The diagnosis this time was crushing. She had a life-threatening infection and needed immediate surgery. The lead doctor had left town and was not reachable, so one of his junior colleagues would have to perform the second procedure. The junior doctor made it clear that the odds were heavily stacked against Mom surviving the operation.

The whole family was devastated, especially Dad. Just as after the car accident ten years prior, he seemed to go into a state of walking shock. His questions and suggestions to the doctors were almost incomprehensible.

Before we made the decision on my mother's behalf to approve the second surgery, the five of us siblings had a family meeting to weigh the pros and cons. We quickly agreed: Mom was going to die if we didn't elect to operate; at least with the surgery, there was a small chance she would live.

We also resolved that it was best for Dad not to sit in the hospital and wait. Once again, I couldn't decide if he or Mom was facing more dire straits. Looking out from a holding room in the hospital at his beloved Baltimore, we realized that the antidote to his anxious state lay there right in front of us. Jeanne and I made a plan to take him on a drive down the memory lanes of his childhood hometown while the doctors tried to save Mom.

First the three of us stopped in the hospital chapel to say

a few prayers. There happened to be a Mass going on. The Gospel reading was about Jesus telling his disciples to "be ready, because the Son of Man will come at an hour when you do not expect." The priest then spoke, saying that we must always be prepared because we don't know when we will meet God. I thought that if today was Mom's last day on earth, if she was going to meet God today, she was prepared. She had given her life to helping people with developmental disabilities; she had raised five kids, all of whom adored her; she had a beautiful marriage; she went to Mass daily, believed in God, and lived the message to love one another. If it had to happen, she was ready, and I felt calmed by that.

We walked out of the chapel with Dad, got into the car, and drove around Baltimore. When I'd lived in the city, I had come to know the cardinal of Baltimore, William Keeler, fairly well. Now I called his office and asked if he was available for a short visit. He was; we headed over to the Basilica of the Assumption, which served as Cardinal Keeler's church and residence. It had been built between 1806 and 1821, as the first cathedral in the United States, and it is where Dad's godfather, Cardinal Gibbons, was interred.

Dad's spirits picked up when we went into the cathedral and met the cardinal. All the while, the surgery was taking place at Hopkins. Dad must have felt like Peter Sellers in the movie *Being There*. Famous doctors, me and my siblings, the cardinal—all were talking to him, he spoke back unclearly, but everyone assented and kept engaging him. All the confusion and anger I had felt building toward him dissipated into simple pity. This accomplished man who had bestrode the globe was helpless—Sargent Shriver, helpless!—as his wife was being cut open just a few blocks away.

After a while, we said good-bye to the cardinal and headed over to the great Lexington Market, a collection of food shops under one big roof where Old Bay seasoning, beer, and Italian meats gave off the scents of a foreign land. "I remember coming here as a kid," Dad said. "I was great friends with the owner's son. We used to come here all the time after school. You can get anything you want—from chicken to fish to fresh meats to ice cream and all sorts of treats. I loved the crab cakes at Faidley's—they're the best in Maryland. Actually, they're the best in the United States."

I never forgot the gravity of what was going on, but for a moment I saw Dad light up and breathe deeply, revealing a flickering of his former self.

Back at the hospital, we went straight to the ICU. For the second time in ten years, I watched Dad watching Mom in a hospital bed, and even though she was the one on the edge of death, he looked more like the one about to die. She had tubes going in and coming out all over her, and when Dad saw her, he stopped in his tracks. I looked at him and saw the stains on his pants. Right away, I knew that he had soiled himself. Taking him by the shoulders, I half-carried him to the closest bathroom. I helped clean him, and again I reflected that you don't become a parent to your parents. Yes, you can help them clean up the mess they make, but that is all you have in common with a parent of a young child. Because in this case, you are utterly heartbroken by the spectacle.

Amazingly, Mom came through the second surgery, once again defying the odds. She willed herself through another near-death experience. She was relentless—like those Special Olympics athletes whom she loved to watch compete.

Driving back and forth to Baltimore over the coming days as she recuperated, I just couldn't get that image of Dad out of my mind. My siblings and I realized it was time to assess his decline. One of Dad's friends put us in touch with the head of psychiatry at Hopkins, Paul McHugh. Dr.

McHugh, who was a big admirer of Dad's, had stopped by Mom's room to offer his services prior to the second surgery. I reached out to him during her recovery and asked him to meet with Dad to test him for Alzheimer's. It was so ironic: we'd all thought Mom was going to die, and now she was on the mend; but Dad, still so physically strong, was going to be tested for a disease that kills every time.

Dr. McHugh suggested a formal evaluation. I wasn't surprised; in fact, I was relieved. McHugh, this cherubic man, so upbeat and sharp, delivered his suspicion with a calmness that brought me a sudden respite from a decade of denial and doubt. He made me feel the way a great priest or healer makes you feel: not necessarily hopeful about the situation, but hopeful that you will survive it.

So one day on our drive up to Baltimore to visit Mom, with Rags behind the wheel and Dad and I in the back seat, I explained to Dad that Dr. McHugh and some of his associates were going to test his memory. Dad was jovial—he knew that Mom was going to live, and his spirits were high. He liked Dr. McHugh and had no problem with being tested, saying to me, "Look, I know I don't have the same memory I had twenty or thirty years ago. If Dr. McHugh can help me out, I am happy to go see him. This is fine."

In the doctor's waiting room, Dad and I exchanged small talk until his name was called. We both stood up and headed back, but Dr. McHugh gently and politely told me that I did not need to accompany Dad for the testing. Dad smiled and said, "See you later!" There was nothing more for me to do now but wait for the phone call.

The testing revealed that Dad was indeed in the early stages of Alzheimer's. Dr. McHugh prescribed Aricept, a medication that might help slow the progression of the disease but not stop it. And we began our quarterly visits to Hopkins. But we really began the challenge of becoming comfortable

with the art of not knowing. In 2000, no one really understood the nature and complexity of the disease; Aricept
worked in some cases but not in others. We now had a name
for his condition, but naming things alone, we realized, offers
meager consolation. We did know, however, the endgame.
The disease would have its way, and Dad would continue to
disappear. I knew I was headed into that test of my mettle.
And I was skeptical of its strength.

◇

CHAPTER 21

RISE AND FALL

M y cell phone kept buzzing in my pocket the night of the November 2000 congressional elections. I was leaving Johns Hopkins Hospital; Mom was slowly recovering, and I felt momentarily relieved. The first call I took, in the parking lot, was from a friend who told me that longtime Kennedy friend Terry Lierman had lost by a few percentage points to eight-term incumbent Republican Connie Morella in Maryland's Eighth Congressional District. I not only lived in the Eighth District but had been born and raised there as well. And Maryland's Legislative District 15, the one I had represented for six years in the Maryland House of Delegates, was in the Eighth Congressional District.

The next day, the phone calls continued. Countless people told me that if I was ever going to run for the U.S. House of Representatives, 2002—the next election—was the year to do it. Morella was obviously vulnerable to a well-financed, well-run campaign, and the 2000 census meant that the district was going to be redrawn. If I wanted to run, I had to get to work immediately. I'd have to persuade Terry not to run again, convince all other Democrats not to challenge me in the primary, encourage the Democratic governor, Parris

Glendening, and the Democratic political leadership in the House and Senate to make the district even more Democratic, and put together a committee that would raise money (and also scare off any challengers). I also had to get ready for the 2001 legislative session in Annapolis, which would begin in just a few weeks, in early January.

And I had two young children at home, a sick mother—and a dad with early Alzheimer's.

Looking back, I can't help but wonder—*What the hell were you thinking, contemplating a run for Congress with all that other stuff going on?* Any sane person would have skipped the race and focused on the family issues.

But that old Kennedy competitive bug to be a big shot on the big stage started buzzing in my mind, and I set out to win. I also think denial played a big role—I was denying that Dad was really sick. He was still going to the office on a daily basis, and he was still giving great speeches, even if they wandered. Mom was on the mend, their house was almost finished, and Jeanne was a great mother to our two young kids. I could balance it all, right?

I've often marveled at how Mom moved the family into the American embassy in Paris in May 1968, then flew back to America for Uncle Bobby's funeral in early June, flew back to Paris, and then, in Chicago six weeks later, staged the first International Special Olympics Summer Games. As she criss-crossed the Atlantic Ocean, she must have experienced joy and excitement and great sadness. I know that she was pulled in different directions—I heard that in the car on the way to the Games, when she realized that she didn't have a bathing suit, she stopped at Sears to buy one so she could swim with the athletes in a portable pool that had been set up in the middle of Soldier Field.

If she could march on in the midst of such tragedy, surely I could handle this situation. I'd been taught to believe that the best thing to do in trying times is to keep moving, doing something—anything, really—and everything will work out.

So I went full bore into the congressional race. But as I put together my committee for my congressional run and hired staff, the pressure began to build. Chris Van Hollen, a well-respected state senator and a formidable candidate, entered the race. Ira Shapiro, an esteemed senior-level State Department employee, also decided to run. The district was heavily Jewish, and Ira had an impressive résumé. Now I faced two serious opponents. And to top it off, the *Washington Post* pinpointed our race as the "national race of the year," which meant that its editors would use it as a national case study on the vulnerability of moderate Republicans such as Connie Morella and the impact of redistricting. Moreover, the allure of a scion of the Kennedy family in the race drove the *Post*'s coverage. Of course, any whiff of Kennedy competition spurred me to push myself as hard as I could—and, as I would come to see, far more than I should.

◇

The race intensified with each passing day. I hired a talented political consultant from Chicago named David Axelrod and his colleague David Plouffe. They had worked with my cousin Congressman Patrick Kennedy on his races, and Axelrod had a daughter with epilepsy; thus they understood how to work with the family, and Axelrod had a personal connection with my parents' commitment to people with developmental disabilities. All of my friends from Chicago knew of Axelrod and spoke highly of him. It didn't matter that he was also working with an Illinois state senator named Barack Obama, who was thinking of running for the U.S. Senate in 2004.

In addition, I brought on a senior-level campaign manager, Mike Henry, who had run high-profile races before, including a successful U.S. Senate race in Florida and two congressional races, both of which he'd won. In 2008 he would be named deputy campaign manager for Hillary Clinton's presidential race. And Steve Neill, my campaign manager for the two House of Delegates races, was on board to run field operations under Mike's direction.

Staff and consultants cost money. A lot of money. So the fund-raising went into overdrive. Both Van Hollen and Shapiro started to assemble top-quality staff and consultants, too, and though I raised more money than they did, they each amassed considerable sums and were not scared out of the race.

The pressure got worse.

And Dad got worse, slowly but surely.

During the 1994 campaign, Dad had driven himself around most of the time; in the 1998 campaign, Rags had chauffeured him regularly; but in the 2002 campaign, I had to assign a full-time volunteer to drive Dad and accompany him for canvassing and other activities. Rags was still working for my parents, but he was eighty years old and showing signs of slipping, too. He would forget to bring Dad to events, and they would show up late for others.

When Dad came to the office to help out, I would give him a list of people to call to ask for money, but I'd have to walk him through the task multiple times. If he wanted to go knock on doors, he came back at the end of the day having met only four or five people and knocked on seven or eight doors. I knew that those four or five people would vote for me and put up a lawn sign but, God, there was no way I was going to win a congressional election four or five people at a time. I knew how much he could have helped if he were only healthy; that compounded the frustration. I became irritable around Dad; I didn't want to criticize him, but I could hardly tolerate his behavior.

On the home front, the initial quirks of Alzheimer's were turning into annoying compulsions. Though the doctors will tell you that no two cases of Alzheimer's are alike, repetitive behavior is one of the common symptoms. Dad insisted that every light in their home be turned on at the beginning of the day and stay on until he went to bed. He would also wander through the house flipping lights off and on to make sure they were not only on but turned up as brightly as possible. I would go over to see Mom and Dad after a long day of campaigning and the house would be ablaze with light. It was a horrible waste of electricity, but when I tried to turn down the lights or even shut them off, Dad would follow behind me and flip them back on. His fixation with the lights irritated me; its larger significance was ripping me apart.

When I escaped to the Cape for a few days, another strange habit worsened: Dad insisted that all of the windows in the house be shut and locked throughout the day and night. One of the great joys of Cape Cod is the cool ocean breeze, so Dad's latest obsession was more than an annoyance; the house was hotter than hell but he kept moving around closing any windows I had opened.

Although he was slowly declining, he nonetheless continued to send me daily letters. They rambled a bit more than in the past, but it was still wonderful to arrive home and find an envelope with his name on the back. In late September 2001, I got home exhausted after another day on the campaign trail, and opened his letter and read:

Dear Jeanne and Mark,
Once again this morning, I was admiring the enchanting holiday photo of Molly and Tommy that you sent me this

past Christmas. I have to say that nobody, not even you two, deserves such a beautiful daughter and an aggressively attractive young son.

Wow, wow, wow, you lucky duo!

Even if you get elected, I highly recommend you continue the procreation track on which you have received such extraordinary results. Molly and Tommy will be well prepared to take charge of two more or maybe even four more! If you actually had four more, you could both gloat once again by emphasizing to your parents that you have exceeded them both in human procreation as well as in political power.

Love,

Dad

Despite wonderful notes like this, the campaign kept grinding along, and by the beginning of the summer of 2002, I felt beaten. I had been in campaign mode since November 2000—almost twenty months of nonstop action. My poll numbers had slipped and now showed that I was in a dead heat with Van Hollen. I was told that I needed to raise more money each and every day. Kathleen Kennedy Townsend was running for governor, and both the local and the national press were saying that two Kennedys in Maryland was one too many. The prospect of losing the primary looked very real, and the humiliation of the potential defeat started to eat at me. And it made me even less patient with Dad.

I remember going over to visit Mom and Dad on a hot and humid June night. My head was filled with all those thoughts, and I knew that I still had work to do when I got home. That meant yet another evening away from Jeanne, Molly, and Tommy, even if I was there with them physically.

I walked into my parents' house. The air conditioner was

either off or broken, and the place was hot and every light was on. I was pissed. I started to turn off the lights, but by the time I had gotten through a few rooms, Dad had come downstairs and begun flicking the lights back on. I couldn't stand it anymore and uncorked my anger on him. "What the hell is the matter with you?" I yelled at him. "This house is huge, and you and Mom are the only two living here. You don't need every light on. You're wasting money. This is absolutely ridiculous. I'm turning these lights off. Don't touch them."

He didn't say a word. He just looked at me and smiled. I turned around and started to turn off other lights. About twenty seconds passed before Dad began walking toward the switches. But before he had taken three steps, I again yelled: "Don't touch those goddamn lights! Leave them off. You're driving everybody crazy. Leave them off!"

I stormed out of the house. Why did he want those lights on, anyway? What the hell was that about? And I knew that if I snuck up to the Cape for a two- or three-day break later that summer—which Mike and Steve were both in favor of, probably sensing my exhaustion—the house would be sweltering and Dad would be closing windows and turning on lights there, too. I was well aware of the absurdity of lights and windows breaking my spirit, but with Alzheimer's, the irrelevant things are what ultimately get you. They are usually the backbreaking straws. I felt my world caving in. And though my love for Dad did not waver, nor my devotion, I felt guilty. After I would leave him I would beat myself up for my anger, for reacting to what I could not control. He never would have done that, I would say to myself. Dad never would have snapped that way.

A wise friend said to me once that anger is not a primary emotion but, rather, a secondary one, a manifestation of a deeper, far trickier problem. I think I knew this even as I was acting out. I couldn't believe that such an active, athletic man was becoming so slow and doddering. I couldn't believe that a brilliant mind couldn't remember what to say on a telephone call soliciting money. I couldn't believe that a man who'd worked for presidents and cardinals but who treated cab drivers and kids just the same as he did those bigwigs was now consumed with turning the lights on and closing the windows.

Instead of facing the issue head-on, I pretty much ignored Dad for the rest of the campaign. When he came into head-quarters to get a list of doors to knock on, I knew he would return at the end of the day with only a handful of votes. I couldn't rely on him for anything more. I had a great group of friends helping to raise money, and Mom was also "dialing for dollars," so that would have to do. I was pushing Dad to the sidelines because I couldn't handle the stress, anxiety, and anger that his behavior brought out in me.

Then Election Day came. It was a close race, but late that night it was finally over. I called Van Hollen and congratulated him. It was too late even to give a concession speech.

I felt like I had let people down, especially my parents and, of course, the people who had worked so hard for my candidacy. College students had taken off a semester or two to join the cause; perhaps a dozen adult volunteers had dedicated hundreds of hours to phone banking and mass mailing. I felt as if I had greatly disappointed each of them. Kennedys were supposed to win, and I was sure they'd been banking on that.

The next day I walked into my headquarters and saw a few people cleaning up the mess. At lunchtime, a group of young volunteers gathered around. There was a lot of crying and hugging. We bought everyone pizza and had some laughs over the pies. But the finality of a race in politics is so stark: up through Election Day, you are working almost twenty-four hours straight; everyone is simultaneously energized and exhausted. By the next day, you have either won and you are planning for the next phase or you have lost and it's over. You don't have money for salaries or even petty cash to pay for snacks. Actually, I was in debt. After the pizza was gone, those volunteers and college students scattered, literally that afternoon, never to gather as a group again. I sat there with Jeanne in an empty campaign headquarters. I should have remembered that airplane ride after Dad's defeat—how he took it all in with equanimity, gave his great speech, said good-bye to his Secret Service agents and staff, and then flew away with his family to take in the sun and water of the Dominican Republic. But I didn't. I just sat there stunned and sad. And angry.

◇

CHAPTER 22

KEEPING SCORE

In the mid-1980s, the Orioles had decided that the aging Memorial Stadium, on Thirty-third Street, was no longer adequate. The state legislature had approved construction of a more luxurious stadium in downtown Baltimore, right off I-95 (making it more convenient for fans from D.C.), which meant that now we did not have to drive through the city to get to a game. It was a much less exciting ride without Dad taking shortcuts all over town, but it still had that special feel of a father-and-son road trip.

Dad and I were in the new stadium together on April 6, 1992, for the first game ever, in which Rick Sutcliffe pitched beautifully. We were there on September 5, 1995, when Cal Ripken Jr. tied Lou Gehrig's streak for consecutive games played. And we were there, together, the next night when he broke the record, cheering him madly when he hit a home run and later as he ran around the field, shaking hands and high-fiving fans. In the middle of the game.

Throughout all of the games Dad and I attended, he would always keep score. When a batter hit a ground ball to Doug DeCinces, our third baseman, and he threw it to Eddie Murray, our first baseman, Dad would immediately write "5/3" on his scorecard. His record keeping was immaculate, which meant that on the drive home, we could relive the game, batter by batter. He loved it so much that when he turned seventy-three, I gave him a leather notebook with hundreds of score sheets so that he could not only keep track of each game but review the games for as long as he lived.

So in April 2003, it seemed natural for me to grab three-year-old Tommy and pick up Dad to drive up I-95 to see the Orioles play the Boston Red Sox. I had started a new job as head of the U.S. Programs at Save the Children. Almost eight months had passed since the election defeat, and I found the new job exciting and different. The trees were blossoming all around the stadium, and the weather was cool but sunny; spring had arrived, I was at a ball game with my son and my father. What could be better?

During the top of the first, I realized that Dad was struggling to keep score—actually, he was struggling to write the names of the players on the scorecard. So I told him who each player was, sometimes spelling their names slowly so that he could write them in. He did a good job recording the action in the first inning but had more difficulty with each ensuing inning. By the fifth, he had jumbled up the scorecard so badly that it was almost impossible to tell who was at bat. When the pitchers changed and pinch hitters were inserted, it got too confusing for him. It was heart-breaking to watch. Here was a man who so loved baseball that he occasionally even drove alone to Baltimore to watch games; sometimes he would call some of his Baltimore-based friends and ask them to join him. A man who always kept a perfect scorecard. A man in his mid-eighties who was now clearly faltering. Yet he never expressed any frustration, never cursed, never complained.

He loved it when Tommy ate cotton candy and dropped his hot dog on the ground. He loved jawboning with his regular neighbors in the seats in front of us, and he still yelled out at the ballplayers standing on first base. A friend stopped by during the game and took a few pictures, which Jeanne had framed for Tommy. The matting is orange and black, the Orioles' colors; there are pictures of Tommy, Dad, and me, with Dad's scorecard right in the middle of the frame. Along with the scorecard are the tickets from the game, so we will always know who the Orioles were playing and the date. Dad's handwriting is elegant despite the smudges and crossed-out names. Tommy has the collage hanging over his bed.

The frustration of the campaign still lingered, but I had forgotten it that day. The sun was out, the dogwoods were in bloom, I was at a ball game with my son and my dad. Alzheimer's took a back seat that day; what a cruel disease it is! Some days, you feel happy and grateful for the day, for the interaction with a loved one. Some days, you dread their company, and the sadness overwhelms you. Some days, you run the gamut of emotions in the span of an hour. But this day showed me that there could still be periods of happiness, especially if I accepted Dad in the moment and didn't compare him to his old self or worry about his future. That's the way he always treated us: he loved us in the moment, for who we were to him—a reminder I sorely needed.

CHAPTER 23

IRELAND

What we'd once called his idiosyncrasies now clearly were becoming his regular behaviors, and they were causing stress at Special Olympics, where Dad was chairman of the board. Mom was honorary chair, and Timmy was CEO. The situation was not tenable for long, as the 11th Special Olympics World Summer Games were scheduled to be held outside the United States for the first time in June 2003. If Dad were to continue as chairman, he would have a very public and prominent role, including giving speeches.

Each of my siblings was experiencing the changes in Dad, but none of us more intensely than Timmy, who was working with him daily. After numerous conversations with Mom, Timmy approached Dad about resigning as chairman. Dad agreed, and they determined that the best way to announce the news would be to write a letter to his friends about the departure and, at the same time, inform them that he was suffering from Alzheimer's. So in April 2003, Dad sent a note to a couple hundred friends doing just that. He explained that he was excited to focus on the next chapter in his life, though Alzheimer's was clearly going to impinge on his abilities. The tone was positive and upbeat, and at the end he wrote:

I look forward to being in touch with as many of you as possible. If names are slow to come to me, please forgive me. But if, at any moment, I seem content with things as they are, don't leave the room. Remind me of the great times we've had and of the great work waiting to be done. I'm sure I'll be eager to rise to face new challenges, whatever they may be.

Within a few weeks, we were all headed to Ireland for the first Special Olympics World Summer Games held on foreign soil. The sense of déjà vu was startling: Mom, pregnant with me, had accompanied Uncle Jack on his trip to Ireland as president in 1963. Now, forty years later, the games were being held in her family's homeland, and she was energized. And I loved Ireland, too, having visited twice before and played rugby there when I was in college.

The opening ceremony was held in Croke Park, and I don't think I have been in a more raucous stadium in my life. Yes, the stadium at Louisiana State University in 1983 shook, but when I walked into Croke Park, the place felt like its own electric storm.

Before the ceremony started, the sixty-five thousand fans spontaneously broke out into song. The procession of more than seven thousand athletes from 150 countries only electrified the place more. When the lights dimmed and U2 started playing "One," I thought the stadium was going to explode. Then they began another song, "Pride (In the Name of Love)." Toward the end of the song, as the band continued to play, Bono walked backstage; he reemerged holding the hand of Nelson Mandela.

The place erupted. U2 finished the song and Bono said, "This is the president not just of South Africa. This is the president of . . . everyone who loves and fights for freedom. Nelson Mandela." Mandela officially opened the games and was joined onstage by Mom and Dad and the other celebrities on hand as the music blared and the place erupted again.

We didn't get back to the hotel until two-thirty in the morning. We were up and out by eight-thirty A.M. for a full day of activities. That meant Mom and Dad were up and out, too. Actually, they were up and out before the rest of us.

That evening, the Special Olympics Board of Directors held a dinner party at Dublin Castle. The Taoiseach (Ireland's prime minister), Bertie Ahern, was there, along with other prominent Irish political and business leaders, as well as Olympic athletes, such as Bart Conner and Nadia Comaneci, all of whom were there to support Special Olympics. A video made in Dad's honor would be shown, and afterward he would speak. Given the level of activity leading up to the dinner, his age, his Alzheimer's, and the time of night, I was nervous that Dad was going to embarrass himself.

He had developed the habit, over the years, of having his speeches typed out on small index cards. After the video was shown, Dad rose and walked over to the lectern, cards in hand. Dessert had been served, but I couldn't eat. I fidgeted with my fork and felt uneasy in the pit of my stomach, terrified that Dad would lose track of those small cards or wander off on an incomprehensible tangent.

But his words once again startled me. He said:

Thank you, Taoiseach, for your warm words.

    On behalf of the members of the Board of Directors of Special Olympics International, I want to say how pleased we are that the first Special Olympics World Summer Games of this, the twenty-first century, are being held in your beautiful country.

    My special thanks to Stacey and John for their eloquent introduction of that marvelous video.

What a joy it was for me to view this film! I could see once again many of the faces of those I met as I traveled around the globe over these last three and one half decades to deliver the message of Special Olympics.

Last evening we witnessed the pageantry of the opening ceremonies. Most impressive of all, we saw seven thousand Special Olympics athletes march into Croke Park, all proud to participate in these games, proud to do their best, and proud to show the world what persons with mental retardation can do!

At the beginning of the last century, that would have been impossible. But Special Olympics athletes have opened up the minds and hearts of people all over the globe. The capabilities of persons with mental retardation have been revealed everywhere for the first time in all of human history!

So, as we gather tonight in this, the third year of the twenty-first century, we all must look forward, not backward. I, for one, hope and pray that we all shall continue to reach out to all families and athletes everywhere.

Let us work together and pray that, together, we can make the twenty-first century the first century in human history where all persons of all colors, of all intellectual abilities, of all physical abilities, of all economic realities are united! May we produce the first generation of human beings living together everywhere without prejudice!

But that cannot happen, I fear, unless all of us individually and collectively, in all nations, and in all places, large and small, work together, play together, and pray together.

When he finished, the room exploded in a standing ovation. There he was, an eighty-seven-year-old man with Alzheimer's, a man who had stayed up late the night before, who had traveled across the Atlantic to cheer on athletes with developmental disabilities from all over the world. It was his swan song as chairman, and he didn't mention all that he had achieved—he barely spoke about himself! He asked us all to work together to create a future without war and without prejudice. And his faith and hope and love shone through—he was hopeful for the future but only if we worked and played together and, of course, prayed together.

Even as he struggled with his memory and his mind faltered, he was, at his core, the same human being, breaking his mirror so as not to focus on himself, hopeful about humanity and the years ahead despite knowing the trials that lay ahead for him personally, and loving everyone, especially those society had shunned the most.

A constant other-centeredness. He never lost it.

◇

CHAPTER 24

FAREWELL, FRIEND

I remember one of the last times I saw them together. It was at eighty-thirty A.M. Mass in the chapel of Our Lady of Mercy, a small, intimate setting adjacent to the large church, where Dad went for Sunday Mass.

I was on time, surprisingly, and they were five minutes late, which was also a surprise. Dad was late for everything in his life, but he was almost always on time for Mass. Not today, though, not when he was eighty-nine and Rags was eighty-two. But they got there.

As was their usual routine, Dad sat in a chair in the second-to-last row while Rags stood at the back of the chapel. Neither one saw me standing in the rear corner, about twenty feet away from them.

Early morning Masses are quick—twenty to twenty-five minutes, tops. Before I knew it, we were headed to the consecration of the Eucharist, which requires one to kneel down.

For a number of years, Dad had suffered from a painful knee. His kneecap had been replaced, but it had never healed correctly. He limped occasionally and complained less.

As I pulled out the kneeler in front of me, I glanced over to check on Dad. He was the last person standing upright in that little chapel. He was looking down at the kneeler. He had Alzheimer's, but he knew that he was supposed to kneel. I could see his right leg kicking at the kneeler, trying to get it to go down. Bending low enough to pull the kneeler down would hurt his knees, so he was trying to jimmy it down with his leg.

Then, out of the corner of my eye, I saw Rags on the move. He quietly slipped into Dad's row.

He pulled down the kneeler and held Dad's arm. He pointed at it and whispered something into Dad's ear. Dad immediately started to bend down, with Rags's arm helping him.

He knelt, but before Rags could return to the back of the chapel, Dad grabbed his arm one last time. He looked Rags in the eye and mouthed the words "Thank you. God bless you." Rags mouthed "God bless you, too, Mr. Shriver" and slipped out of the pew.

◇

One of the most heartbreaking moments of my life occurred not long after that. I had to tell Rags, after almost forty years of service, that with Dad's condition continuing to deteriorate, the family had decided that he needed a full-time aide experienced in dealing with Alzheimer's. That meant that the new person would also drive Dad everywhere. I knew that Rags saw himself, above all, as Dad's right-hand man—his "Top Man"; he loved being the one who got Sargent Shriver where he needed to go to make the world a better place, and driving him there was a big part of the job.

When I finally found the right man for the job—a thirty-year-old fellow who had been an aide to a former ambassador who had suffered from Alzheimer's—I had to tell Rags that his days of driving Dad full-time were really and truly over.

When we spoke about the change, I told Rags the truth: he had done so much for Dad, and for all of us, but Dad needed more support than either he or I could provide. He was always welcome at the house, but John, the new guy, needed to assume most of Rags's heavy workload.

Rags was stubborn. "Markie," he replied, "when your grandma Shriver was on her deathbed, she asked me to take care of your dad until he died—or I died. I promised her I would, and I am not going to stop now."

I cringed. A deathbed promise was hard to break, especially for a man as loyal as Rags. When I insisted that Dad needed John's additional support, Rags got angry and told me that he quit. It wasn't the first time he had done this routine, but in the past he would always come back to work the next day. It was almost comical—he'd get angry at Mom, or vice versa. Rags would "quit" or Mom would "fire" him, and the next day, he'd be back at the house as if nothing had happened. This time was different. He stayed away for a couple of weeks and then called me.

"I think I'll come to work tomorrow, Markie," he said. "Come see your dad and drive your mom to the office. I gotta run a few errands for your mom—gotta pick up her medicine—and I gotta check on things at the house. And I'll help that new guy, John. He's a good guy, and I want to help him learn the ropes, you know what I mean?"

I told him he was always welcome at the house. Anytime. We loved him. He came that next day, and he came back again after that. But he didn't come every day. We had other people helping my parents, but no one replaced Rags; he was irreplaceable. People drove Dad to the office, around town, to events, but no one loved Dad like Rags did. No one cared for him like Rags did. Having a hand in breaking up their partnership upset me as much as anything that happened as a result of the disease. Before, my anger and hurt had arisen out of frustration and self-pity—why was this happening to *my* father? But now this creeping disease was forcing me to take steps that hurt other people. I felt like I was sending Rags off to die.

◇

CHAPTER 25

FUN AND GAMES

As the Alzheimer's relentlessly advanced through the mid-2000s, Jeanne, the kids, and I would try to go to my parents' house for dinner at least one night a week. Often we would go the same night as Timmy and Linda and their kids. The kids loved being together, and their energy, in turn, energized Mom and Dad.

On a typical Sunday, we would join Mom and Dad at ten forty-five Mass and then eat brunch at their house. Timmy and Linda and their gang would join us around two or three for games like Capture the Flag or tennis or water polo or pepper. Dad didn't actively participate, but he would walk out to the court or the big field that was their backyard and sit and watch. He'd yell a few words of encouragement and wave and smile.

Mom would play the games as best she could. In Capture the Flag, she'd stay on the line and yell when an opposing player dashed for the flag. She'd explain to Dad what was going on—and then, when everyone was focused elsewhere, she would run for the flag.

In her prime, Mom was fast. And when I say "prime," I mean until she hit her early seventies. The big car crash in 1990 had slowed her down a step or two, and a few years later, on the Cape, she'd been involved in another accident. A young kid hit her head-on and, once again, she had to be taken to the hospital, this time with a broken leg. That, too, took a toll.

But on the weekends, when the grandkids visited, she wanted to play, and play she did.

Her bursts for the goal were never successful, but she would laugh and scream as she ran. Inevitably, one of the littlest kids—Molly or Tommy or Timmy's daughters Caroline and Kathleen—would tag her. She would express shock and disappointment, most of it an act (though I knew there was at least a little truth to her look of disappointment, too), while the grandkids screamed with delight. Dad would yell something like "Nice try, Eunie baby!"

When she was freed from "jail," the routine would start all over again.

In the pool, when a water basketball game would start, Mom always wanted to play. Those games would get rough quickly—there was plenty of shoving and pushing and dunking one's opponent—but when Mom had the ball, you were not allowed to touch her. She'd shoot and then let out a cry of victory or anguish, depending on the results.

Dad would sit by the pool and yell his encouragement, often getting into the pool to swim and take a few jump shots, but he rarely participated in the games anymore.

Then off to dinner we would all go. It was during dinner conversations that Dad increasingly struggled to keep up.

Mom always liked to maintain big, table-wide conversations. She dutifully included Dad, insisting that even the grandkids address him. She would ask Dad for his opinion on the issue being discussed. She'd say, "Well, Sarge, what do you think of Timmy's point?" or "What do you say about that, Sargie?"

As Dad's Alzheimer's advanced, his answers became

shorter and less coherent. Sometimes he'd come up with a few words that offered a profound insight, but as the disease moved along, those insights waned. Yet Mom always asked for his input. Sometimes she demanded it of him.

I often got frustrated by their question-and-answer routine, thinking how foolish she was for asking so much of him. Couldn't she see that he was slipping? Was she trying to embarrass him? Wasn't it as frustrating for her as it was for the rest of us to see him fading away? Why shine a light on it?

My frustration extended to phone calls, too. When I called to say hello, Mom always grabbed Dad and put him on the phone. He didn't know which end to speak into, and when he did figure it out, the conversations were short.

I often visualized what their dinners were like when it was just the two of them sitting at that big table. I had a pretty good idea, as I would stop by the house on occasion to say hi or pick something up.

They would be eating next to each other at one end— the end where Mom always sat. I could hear their conversation from the hallway, and then I'd enter the dining room. They'd smile, inquire about the kids, and ask me to join them. We'd chat for a bit, and then I'd tell them that I had to head home. They'd ask me to stay, but my excuse was a good one: I wanted to get home to be with Jeanne and the kids.

Whenever I left, I always felt that they must be lonely in such a huge house, especially two people who so loved action and whose homes had always been filled with friends, Peace Corps staffers, Special Olympics athletes, and animals of all shapes and sizes and numbers. They had built their final home, the "big house," when all of us kids had moved out; they'd built it so we would all come back and fill it with our own kids and causes. It must have hosted three large-scale (750-plus people) fund-raisers annually until the year Mom died.

But love conquered their loneliness. Mom loved Dad, and after seven years of courtship, when the cardinal had asked, "Do you take this man in good times and in bad?" and she'd answered yes, she'd meant yes. Mom had made the sacramental commitment to be there in good times and in bad. She had a lifelong partner she wasn't going to abandon, either physically or emotionally. He had been involved in every major decision she had made for more than sixty years. They had been through great highs and great lows, through triumphs and disasters. As they headed down the home stretch of what would be the last six years, dealing with Alzheimer's and car accidents and children who fled the coop, of times that were filled with loneliness and sadness, they loved as if their lives depended on it.

I remember sitting next to Dad one time at the dining room table. After a rare moment of silence, he turned to me and pointed at Mom and said, "Nowadays, everyone wants to change what God has given them. Look at those wrinkles on your mother's face. Have you ever seen a more beautiful woman in your life?"

Mom had a lot of wrinkles. Her hair was often unkempt, and her outfits didn't always match. Dad was old and doddering and suffering from a disease that was eroding one of the most brilliant minds ever. Yet they looked beyond all that and saw a person they loved.

What a marriage.

What a love affair.

We spent many Christmas vacations in Palm Beach with Grandma Kennedy. The mid-1970s were not a great time for fashion—although Grandma Kennedy looks great. (SHRIVER FAMILY COLLECTION)

On the front yard in Hyannis Port. The '70s fashion trends continue! (KEN REGAN/CAMERA 5)

Dad and Senator George McGovern on the campaign trail in August 1972. By most accounts, Dad was McGovern's seventh pick for vice president; he was not embarrassed about that and referred to the seven of us—his wife, his children and himself—as the Lucky 7. (TED POWERS/ ASOCIATED PRESS)

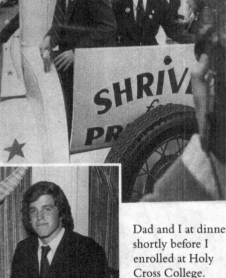

Anthony and I in the back of a Model-T campaigning for Dad in 1976. (DOUG BRUCE)

Dad and I at dinner shortly before I enrolled at Holy Cross College. (LUCIEN CAPEHART PHOTOGRAPHY)

Mom and Dad cheer on Special Olympics athletes at the opening of the 3rd International Special Olympics Winter Games in Park City, Utah, in 1985. (SPECIAL OLYMPICS)

Graduation day, May 1986, Holy Cross College. Dad received an honorary degree that day and was onstage when I received my diploma. (COLLEGE OF THE HOLY CROSS PHOTO ARCHIVES)

Jeanne and I
were married on
June 26, 1992, in
Newport, Rhode
Island. Mom is
standing to my
left, applauding.
(DENIS REGGIE/
SHRIVER FAMILY
COLLECTION)

Here we are at Yale on May 22, 1994, one day before Mom and Dad's
forty-first wedding anniversary. From left are: Alina, Anthony, Dad,
Bobby, Mom, Maria, me, Jeanne, Linda, and Timmy. It's always a battle
to get in the front row of a family photo—nice job, Jeanne and Alina!
(SHRIVER FAMILY COLLECTION)

Dad received the Presidential Medal of Freedom in August 1994. Mom and Dad were the first husband and wife to receive Presidential Medals of Freedom for different bodies of work. (SHRIVER FAMILY COLLECTION)

Dad sent this photo to the five of us some ten years later with the following note:

SARGENT SHRIVER
1325 G STREET NW, SUITE 500
WASHINGTON, DC 20005

March 25, 2004

Dear Bobby, Maria, Timothy, Mark and Anthony:

I thought this photograph taken of your Mother and me at the White House on August 4,1994 when President Clinton presented me with the Presidential Medal of Freedom is a very good one.

I remember what a joy it was for me to have your Mother and you with me at this Ceremony. It was truly a wonderful day for me because you all were there.

Love,

Mom and Molly having a blast with a U.S. mail container! (SHRIVER FAMILY COLLECTION)

Dad was a regular volunteer on my 2002 Congressional campaign. (NEIL GRAUER)

Dad, Tommy, and me at the Baltimore Orioles–Boston Red Sox game in April 2003. (NEIL GRAUER)

Mom and Dad at his birthday party. He was a lifelong fan of the Baltimore Orioles and proudly wore his birthday present, an Orioles jersey. (SHRIVER FAMILY COLLECTION)

Here are Mom and Dad after dinner one Sunday night with Tommy, Kathleen, Caroline, Molly, Sam, and Timbo. (SHRIVER FAMILY COLLECTION)

Dad and Rags getting ready for a Best Buddies event. (LAURENCE L. LEVIN)

Emma Rose joined our family on February 18, 2005. Here we are at her baptism. From left: Dad, Jeanne, Emma (in Jeanne's arms), me, Tommy, Molly, Mom, and Jeanne's mother, Libby Scruggs. (LAURENCE L. LEVIN)

A summer weekend in Hyannis Port. Front row: Molly, Caroline, Mom, Dad, Tommy and me; second row: Carolina, Katherine, Christina, Malissa, Bobby, Linda, Timmy, Emma, Jeanne, Timbo and Maria; third row: Christopher, Alina, Chessy, Rosie, Patrick, Anthony, Eunie, Kathleen, Sam and Natasha. Only Teddy is missing (Joey and Rosemary were not yet born)! (LAURENCE L. LEVIN)

The Lucky 7 at Mom's eighty-fifth birthday. Standing behind Mom and Dad, from left, are Bobby, Maria, Anthony, Timmy and me. (LAURENCE L. LEVIN)

◇

CHAPTER 26

I WILL YELL NO MORE

A doctor once told Maria something that really stuck with me: Once you've seen one case of Alzheimer's, you've seen . . . one case of Alzheimer's. The disease fluctuates so aggressively that your own loved one is a different person on each visit, too.

So, I thought: once you've seen one day of Alzheimer's, you've seen . . . one day of Alzheimer's. The multiple feelings that the disease elicits make for an unthinkable roller coaster, and I, at least, felt like I was rising and falling and twisting and turning each day of Dad's illness. Doubt, anger, sadness: pick your poison, depending on the day.

There were still many moments of happiness with Dad, especially when the latest addition to our family, a beautiful baby girl, Emma Rose Shriver, was born, on February 18, 2005. Dad didn't come bursting into the hospital room this time, but before too long Emma was playing games with both Mom and Dad. Both of them developed a strong bond with her, a bond that was deepened by Emma's medical problems.

At eighteen months of age, Emma complained a lot about a stomachache. When Tommy and Molly told Jeanne that Emma had played a game of jacks and now they couldn't find one of the jacks, Jeanne took Emma to the pediatrician. The doctor thought there was little chance that Emma had swallowed the piece but recommended an X-ray just to be safe. The X-ray showed that Emma hadn't swallowed the toy, but it did show that she had gallstones. The doctor was very surprised, as gallstones are exceedingly rare for an eighteen-month-old. Soon we were headed to surgery with our youngest.

Mom was her usual self, telling us, "Don't worry. She is wonderful and strong. I have never seen a brighter, stronger kid in my life. She'll be fine." Typical Mom—strong-willed and positive. If she was concerned, she wasn't going to let it show.

I think Dad couldn't quite figure out what gallstones were and why Emma needed surgery. But the day before her surgery, when we took Emma to visit him, he gave her a big hug and a kiss and said, "You will be great! God loves you, and so do I."

Emma came through the operation well and was over at the "big house" in a few weeks. And the first thing she did on that visit was the same thing she had done in the past: she ran into the house and screamed, "Grandma! Grandpa!" She kicked off her shoes and barreled up the stairs, straight to Mom's room. She gave her a big kiss on the lips and then grabbed her hand and kissed that, too. Together they played with the dolls in Mom's room.

And then she headed out back to play with Dad. They threw a tennis ball and kicked a soccer ball around. Dad pretended to throw her the ball one way and then tossed it in a different direction, to Molly. And then he laughed. His mind was failing, but he still knew how to give a head fake.

Despite the fact that both Mom and Dad were slowing down, the kids still loved to visit them. There was less commotion and fewer people around than when I'd grown up, but usually something was going on or someone fun was visiting.

"Let's go to Grandma's house," Emma would yell every day when I'd get home from work. "Let's play in her room and go see Grandpa."

◇

One day I picked up Dad and took him to one of Molly's lacrosse games.

Molly is our oldest child, and that competition gene ensured that I was not going to let her lag behind her friends or cousins. Just as I'd wanted to win as a kid, I drove Molly to succeed. I taught her how to play tennis when she was in second grade, always encouraging her to move faster and hit the ball harder.

I knew that she'd never play at Wimbledon—I mean, seriously, how many kids ever make it to pro sports?—but I still thought that she should learn to hustle. Hustling on a tennis court meant that she'd learn to hustle in life, too, correct? I thought that it was important for her to understand that she needed to be competitive, especially in the suburbs of Washington, where everyone was so preoccupied with the talents and successes of young people.

My mom and dad pushed themselves relentlessly, never missing a day of work. When something bad happened, their response was simple: Pick yourself up and go right back at it. So I pushed because I thought it was the right thing to do, not only for a victory on the tennis court but also to get Molly prepared for the competition that is life.

Sometimes when I looked around at my friends, I felt that we weren't pushing Molly hard enough. It seemed as if every one of Molly's friends played on a school team and on at least one other team. Some played on two other teams. And when I spoke to my college friends who were spread across the country, the stories were the same: push, push, push!

When Molly was ten years old, she started playing lacrosse. I pushed her just as hard as I had in tennis, playing catch and running drills with her in the backyard.

One day, during a lacrosse game, I saw Molly chatting away with the opposing team's goalie. During the middle of the game! I couldn't believe it.

After the game, as we walked to the car, I nonchalantly asked Molly, "What were you doing out there talking to the goalie? That's the person you want to score on, honey—you've got to throw the ball at the girl's feet or at her. You've got to score on that girl, not chat with her."

Molly smiled and said, "The ball was on the other side of the field for so long. I asked her her name and where she went to school. I know some kids that go to school with her. She was really nice. I'm going to try to meet up with her next weekend."

I couldn't believe it—Molly wanted to meet the goalie next weekend to have fun?! I held back and said something like "Oh, that's nice" and let it pass.

The day Dad came to her lacrosse game, he sat smiling and marveling at the scene in front of him: young people in the prime of their lives excelling at a sport on a gorgeous day. That is what he would have thought ten years prior, I knew, but now I assumed he just sat there smiling because the sun was warm on his face and he was with us.

I, on the other hand, was constantly yelling instructions.

About halfway through the first half, Dad suddenly said to me, "Hey there."

I looked at him. He wasn't smiling, and I became instantly alarmed that something bad was happening.

He looked straight at me.

"You're yelling a lot," he said.

"I know, Dad," I said, relieved that there wasn't a crisis. "This is a really close game. Molly has to move or else we could lose."

I turned around and yelled again.

A minute or two passed before he said, "Hey there. Did I yell like that at you, too?"

I looked at him. He hadn't spoken in an accusatory tone. His face was not expressing anger. It was just a matter-of-fact question. I was stunned. Had he suddenly remembered that I was his son? I thought that connection had left his mind years ago. Did he fully understand what yelling meant? Did he know Molly was my daughter, his granddaughter? I didn't think he had that cognitive capacity anymore. He looked at me for what must have been five seconds but seemed like an eternity. He smiled ever so slightly.

"Did I?" he asked again, never once raising his voice or changing its tone.

I didn't answer. *Of course you didn't, Dad,* I thought. Even when I was getting crushed in high school tennis, he'd never said a negative word. Even when I didn't start for the first three games of my senior year on the Georgetown Prep high school football team, he'd never yelled or expressed disappointment. And when I'd started the final six games and even scored a touchdown against one of our biggest rivals, Gonzaga, Dad had expressed his joy but had never gone overboard. He knew sports were important but not the most important thing in our lives.

"No, you didn't," I said to him. He smiled.

"Good," he said and turned back to resume watching the game and smiling in the sunlight.

What just happened? I asked myself. Was he telling me not to yell? Was that a moment of insight, of clarity, of him being my father again, or were they just random words?

As we drove home, Dad again disappeared into that far-off Alzheimer's land. I tried to engage him, to see if he could come back one more time and be there with us, but he didn't bite. Instead, I talked with Molly—praised her and analyzed certain plays with her.

It was the best postgame trip home we had ever had.

◇

There were other wonderful moments with Dad, but they were usually tinged with sadness. I continually wished that our kids and Jeanne could have experienced Dad at his height, not just seen glimpses of his amazing goodness here and there. They would never be able to know him the way I did.

The emotional roller coaster that comes with Alzheimer's stirred up other emotions. The election campaign and loss still stung. My job at Save the Children was going well, but it required a full-scale overhaul of the program, including a reorganization that meant letting go of dozens of staffers. I was on the road constantly, and I hated that I was missing too much of Molly, Tommy, and Emma's childhoods. And Emma's health was of great concern—shortly after the gallstones operation, she'd had a major infection and then been diagnosed with scoliosis of the back. She was tough and thriving, but it was exhausting.

What's more, I didn't see myself fulfilling that old Kennedy push to be a great man on the big stage.

But perhaps the most draining stress I felt was the gnawing sense that I should be doing more for Dad. I was "in charge" of his medical care and financial matters, but I wasn't really his caregiver. I wasn't in his room waking him up every morning, helping him shave, helping him dress, and cleaning up after him. I wanted to do those things, but, frankly, I didn't have the courage.

And that lack of courage bugged the hell out of me.

Finally, one morning I woke up and looked at the photos of Dad around my room, and I knew what I had to do. At least, I knew what he would have done.

The first Mass, the seven A.M. Mass, was his daily service.

I felt him there as I walked in. I subconsciously imitated his churchly demeanor—not pious but calm, focused, businesslike. Serious business.

As the priest gave his homily, I started to really think about why I was sometimes angry at work: Was it because I believed we were investing more money to eradicate poverty abroad than in the United States? Or was it that I wasn't doing great things like my siblings? Bobby had started Product Red and the One Campaign, with Bono no less. Maria was an accomplished journalist and author who brilliantly raised four children while serving on the board of Special Olympics and running the Women's Conference, which was attended by over thirty thousand people annually. Timmy was CEO of Special Olympics. Anthony had founded Best Buddies and had grown it to fifty countries and fifteen hundred schools. Maria and Timmy had started an ice-cream company called Lovin' Scoopful that was generating money for Special Olympics.

I also couldn't get my head around why I occasionally lost my temper with my kids. I didn't remember my dad once yelling at my siblings or me. I didn't remember him yelling at my mother. If they had disagreements, and I'm sure that they did, they settled them behind closed doors. He worked hard and expected others to work hard, but he never showed a temper at the office, either.

It's not that he didn't have a right to be angry.

In 1960, he wanted to run for governor of Illinois but instead went to Washington to help his wife's brother start the Peace Corps. He was considered by many to be a likely vice presidential pick in 1964 and 1968 but was passed over.

If you believe some historians, his own in-laws made sure he didn't get that job. Yet I never heard him utter one word of bitterness about those significant slights.

In vino veritas, right? Even when Dad would have a couple of drinks and it was just family, or me with a couple of close friends, he never expressed anger or disappointment.

As I sat in the pew, I remembered something he'd said to me a few years earlier as I was driving him to our house for dinner. We had stopped at a red light. I looked over at him, and he was clear-eyed.

He was having one of those lucid moments that make you, as a loved one of an Alzheimer's victim, forget for a minute or two that this is all really happening.

You can forget about the disease and its toll and confusion and suddenly engage with the same person with whom you conversed profoundly for so many years, until it all started to go haywire. In that moment I wanted to know what I think so many Alzheimer's caregivers crave to understand: Do you know what has become of you? Can you, so lucid now, see how you act when you are not like you are now? Does it make you sad? Does it make you ashamed?

The reprieve right there at the red light was momentary, even illusory. But there for the taking, right in front of me—so obvious that I almost panicked over what to talk about. Do we discuss his beloved baseball? His beloved grandchildren? Me—how I'm doing, how much I miss him?

No. As much out of curiosity as concern, I wanted to talk about him.

"Dad," I said, "you are losing your mind. You know that. How does that make you feel? How are you doing with that?"

"I'm doing the best I can with what God has given me," he said.

In the church, these words came back at me like a punch

in the face. My dad, the rock of the family, had never been in control of anything. Dad knew that he was never in control, and he loved it that way. He let go and let God be in control.

He saw everything in his life as a gift from God, from his earlier trials right down to his Alzheimer's. So many of us in the American culture want to believe we are in control, especially men, who often subscribe to that alpha male role of taking charge of their families and their workplaces. Dad didn't believe any of that. He may have been disappointed, but he didn't let that disappointment linger and turn into anger. He believed that God was in control and that if he wasn't meant to be president or vice president or governor, he was going to do the best he could with the gifts that God did give him.

This latest realization of Dad's faith overwhelmed me. I thought I was a good Catholic; I always went to Mass on Sundays and often during the week. And I was always trying, striving to be a good person. But I was still very much a disciple of the American image—maybe it's a universal image—that to be a man, or *the* man, you must be in charge of everything.

Dad's faith turned this idea on its head. God is in charge and you are nothing more than a pencil in God's hand, as Mother Teresa once described herself.

Dad didn't harbor anger toward anyone, including those who may well have shortchanged his career, because he realized he wasn't in control and neither were they. His faith was real and personal, and it freed him from anger and sadness and filled him with hope and love.

Sitting there—in a church, of all places—I realized that what I lacked was his faithfulness. I just didn't have it. Yet.

◇

CHAPTER 27

SAILING AWAY

For about twenty-five years, Uncle Teddy had owned a sixty-five-foot wooden schooner called the *Mya*, a landmark in Hyannis Port Harbor. The blue hull and the two tall masts were a constant, and everyone in town knew that at twelve-thirty or so every day, Teddy and his wife, Vicki, would walk down the pier with a lunch packed and their two Portuguese Water Dogs in tow.

In 2008, Mom and Dad stayed at the Cape for the entire summer. Teddy had been diagnosed with a brain tumor just a few months earlier, Dad continued to suffer from Alzheimer's, and Mom had experienced a series of small strokes. The last lions were staging their exit from the arena. And, as if to enhance the romantic grandeur of it all, they decided they were all going to go sailing.

Mom was wheeled down the pier, accompanied by Dad walking ever so slowly beside her. They gingerly got into the tender (the put-put boat that would take them to Uncle Teddy's schooner in the harbor). It was a cloudy day with the littlest bit of sun poking through; the breeze was steady but not too strong, and the waves were only two or three feet. Good sailing conditions.

A bit later, Vicki described the scene on the boat to me:

Your father got on the boat and almost immediately started saying that the sail was too slow. There was some wind, but he thought we were going too slowly. He said he wanted to go out on a motorboat, and soon thereafter, he said he was too hot. Your mother sat across from him and must have had eight or nine sweaters on! She told your father to enjoy the sail, that it was an absolutely perfect day. And there was Teddy, right in between the two of them, loving every second of their discussion, goading them with a comment here or there, just to get their blood pressure up.

The wind started to pick up, and it began to drizzle a little bit. The weather got a little cooler. Your mother, who had taken off a few of her sweaters earlier in the trip, asked for them back. She asked for a blanket as well. Your father stopped asking to get on a motorboat. It was a glorious sail.

When the tender came to pick your parents up, your father took his first step to get on it, then stopped, turned around, and said to Teddy and me, "That was such a great sail. What a wonderful day. Thank you for having us." Your father was always a perfect gentleman.

Sitting on the beach, I'd watched the *Mya* leave the harbor and set sail on the Nantucket Sound. The schooner was in full bloom, with three big sails up. It tipped a little to the left, so I could see the blue underside of the boat. Dad, Mom, and Vicki were gathered around Teddy. There was one crew member trimming the sails, but it was the image of the four of them together in the back of the boat, heads bobbing and arms moving, that I will never forget.

At first I tried to imagine what they were talking about, but I forced my brain to shut off—there are things in life we will never know. I just sat there and took in the scene of the four of them, out for a sail on the Nantucket Sound, enjoying God's grandeur, together, one last time.

◇

CHAPTER 28

LAST KISS

We visited Jeanne's mom at Lake George, New York, over the Fourth of July weekend in 2009. We swam in the crystal-clear waters of the lake and hiked through the Adirondacks. During the eight-hour trip home, as Jeanne was driving, I got a call from Timmy telling me that Rags was slipping badly and that if I wanted to speak with him before he died, I should call his house immediately. I hung up the phone and stared straight ahead for a good ten minutes.

Rags was going to die.

His demise had happened so fast. A few months after John started working full-time, Rags stopped coming to the house altogether. And then we got the word that Rags himself had Alzheimer's.

I questioned whether my decision to replace Rags had worsened his illness. Surely his departure wasn't the reason that he'd gotten Alzheimer's, but it couldn't have helped him psychologically, either. I tried to look at it another way: maybe he'd worked longer than he should have and that had delayed the illness's onslaught. But in my heart, I believed I had played a role in his rapid demise.

Timmy and I had worked to create situations where

Rags and Dad could get together. We had arranged lunches downtown and met them at the restaurant. We'd invite a few of their other friends to share the laughs and to keep the conversation moving. Both men were in the throes of the disease, so the conversations were often short and stilted. Even though Dad's diagnosis had come a good five or six years before Rags's, Rags slipped faster and, before too long, was more lost than Dad and couldn't make it downtown anymore.

Now here I was, in a car with the three kids and Jeanne alongside me, yelling into a cell phone. "Rags! Rags! Can you hear me? It's Mark, Rags! I miss you, Top Man, I miss you. You're the best, Richard Franklin Ragsdale. Rags!"

All I could hear on the other line was heavy breathing.

Then Elaine, Rags's wife of nearly sixty-seven years, his best friend, and the person who cared for him every day during his illness, took the receiver and said, "He can hear you, honey. He's nodding his head. He can hear you. Say something again."

"I love you, Rags! You're the top man! You're the best!"

What else could I say? That's all I felt. He was the best—a loyal friend who'd fought for his country, married Elaine when she was seventeen and he was nineteen, stayed married for almost sixty-seven years, lived on the same street and had the same phone number for all those years. When his neighborhood went from all white to predominantly African American, Rags never moved. "Blacks, whites—I don't give a shit what color they are," he said, "just as long as they're good neighbors and nice people." He meant it, and that's the way he lived.

Elaine took the phone back, thanked me for calling, and told me in a steady voice, "He's going to die soon, honey. He's tired. He's going to see God."

I thanked her for sharing Rags with all of us over so many years and told her that I loved him.

He died the next day, July 13, 2009.

◇

A few weeks later, we were in the car again, headed north to visit Mom and Dad in Hyannis Port, when Timmy called and told me that Mom had had a major setback and was in the hospital. She was on a ventilator and probably wasn't going to live another twenty-four hours.

She had survived car crashes, broken bones, and an infection that the doctors had thought would kill her. Her battle against that infection was now a case study at Johns Hopkins Hospital.

She had suffered a series of small strokes over the preceding two years, but just eight months earlier, she had hosted an inauguration party at the "big house," attended by more than five hundred people. She'd come downstairs and chatted with senators, congressmen, and people from all over the United States. She'd struggled to follow the conversation at times, and had had to sit in a chair while people came to her, which was not the way she normally hosted parties, but she'd been there, entertaining those guests.

Just fifteen months before that—in October 2007— Mom had traveled to China for the 12th International Special Olympics Summer Games, held in Shanghai. She'd sat next to President Hu at the opening ceremony, which was attended by eighty thousand people, including more than seven thousand athletes. She went to many of the athletic competitions and gave a speech on Chinese national television. And she found the time to go with her grandkids to bargain-hunt at the knockoff stores in downtown Shanghai. Molly still has the $5 Juicy Couture bag Mom bought her.

She had so much energy and fight—after traveling all the way to China and attending two weeks of competition and activities, she came home for two days before heading to Los Angeles to attend Maria's Women's Conference. She spoke there in front of thirty thousand people and, a few days later, flew to Boston to attend an event in her honor at the John F. Kennedy Presidential Library.

And the year before the trip to China, Mom had broken her hip. On the mend at eighty-five, she'd raced Tommy and a buddy of his, Beau, around the inside of the big house. Tommy and Beau had to run a longer loop through the kitchen and pantry, then through the dining room and den, then back into the front hall, while Mom had to go only through the dining room and den and then to the finish line. She'd set up the race course. It was close; the boys almost knocked her over on one turn—she let out a loud scream—but she won. And then she collapsed into a chair, laughing her head off. And breathing heavily.

The boys yelled at her to race again, and, after catching her breath, she lined up once more and faced off against them.

And won.

Jeanne walked into the "big house" and saw Mom in the chair after her second victory, gasping for air, and thought she was having a heart attack.

Once Jeanne heard the whole story from the boys—who were yelling and screaming the details and accusing Mom of cheating—my wife looked at me, rolled her eyes, and walked out of the room.

Mom sat there, breathing heavily, laughing, and jaw-boning with Tommy and Beau. She didn't give them a third chance.

But at eighty-eight, and after a year and a half of declining health, she was failing, and for the first time in my life, I thought that she was going to die.

We made the rest of the trip safely, arriving in Hyannis Port on August 6, and headed immediately to the hospital.

The next few days were torturous. We would drive from the hospital to the house in Hyannis Port, go swimming in the ocean, and then head back to the hospital. The grandkids all said their good-byes, and we waited and waited.

Mom died in the early hours of August 11, 2009, at Cape Cod Hospital. We issued a statement, gathered our belongings, and went home at about four in the morning.

When I awoke, I walked around in a daze. I went to the funeral home with Anthony and Maria to make sure everything was progressing on that front. I had discussions with Timmy about the readings for the funeral Mass. I spoke to the kids and went back to the funeral home to accompany Mom on her last trip to her house in Hyannis Port. Anthony had taken care of all of the arrangements, and when we carried her coffin into the house, he had made sure that there was a cleared area for her in the living room, overlooking her beloved Nantucket Sound.

That evening, with all of our cousins gathered around, we celebrated a Mass at the house. It was an overflow crowd, including Uncle Teddy and Vicki, who joined us even though Teddy was now seriously ill.

Before the Mass, Dad walked into the room and slowly headed to Mom's coffin. He stopped and stared at her. He then moved his hands toward Mom's waist. Anthony had put rosary beads in Mom's hands, now resting on her stomach. Dad gently lifted her hands apart. He took the rosary, kissed the crucifix, and then placed the crucifix on her lips.

It was their last kiss.

◇

CHAPTER 29

SELLING THE BIG HOUSE

W e had decided to put their home on the market a few months earlier. The "big house" was situated on six acres in Potomac, Maryland, and had ten rooms, a tennis court, and a swimming pool, all of which meant an amazing amount of upkeep and work for the two of them. And as they'd grown older, we'd realized that it was obviously too much.

Anthony and I signed the closing documents for the sale of the house a few days before Mom died. Actually, the title to the home transferred to the new owner at the hour her funeral began. The timing was purely coincidental, but utterly painful.

It took us months to clean out the house, and that provided its daily anguish, too. We sent some things to the Kennedy Library, some to the Shriver homestead, and some to Special Olympics; and my siblings and I kept some personal items.

On the last day, I walked through the house and ended up in Mom's bedroom. There I saw a piece of paper in one of her closets. It was a receipt from Toys "R" Us listing fifteen purchases of the same game. I smiled. And then I cried. Mom had wanted to turn her home into a magical kingdom for her grandchildren, filled with games and toys and excitement and fun. And she'd succeeded not just for our kids but for the Special Olympics athletes who'd played there every summer until the year she died. Mom and Dad had lived in the "big house," but they'd shared it with all of us and with the athletes. Her generosity, just like Dad's love, had always been frantic and full-blown. Leaving the house with all those memories was gut-wrenching. I've talked to many friends with elderly parents, and they all say the same thing: selling the family house is one of the most painful things they've had to do.

Throughout this process, we puzzled over what to do with Dad. He was about to turn ninety-four. Should he move to Florida to be near Anthony and his family? Dad had always loved the Florida sunshine, and the good weather would make day trips easier. Should he move to California and live with or near Bobby or Maria? Or should he stay in Potomac, to be near Timmy and Linda and their kids and Jeanne and me and our kids?

I was torn. Neither Timmy nor I had room for him in our homes, but I didn't want him to leave our area. I didn't want him in an assisted living facility, either. I'd always thought assisted living would not do for either of my parents, but what other option did we have if he was going to stay in the D.C. area?

I also thought it would be great for him to be in Florida. It would be especially great for Anthony, Alina, and their children to spend time with him. But I didn't want him to leave. The same was true of California—it was too far. I fully grasped how much I depended on his presence to animate me, even now, in the midst of his decline. Even now his energy and optimism, his fundamental hopefulness helped pick me up and keep me up. I needed him still.

There was no clear answer, just a lot of confusion and guilt.

After numerous family conversations, Jeanne and I checked out a few assisted living facilities. We found a place just a couple of miles from my parents' home. The facility itself was beautiful; it looked like a ski lodge nestled in the Colorado Rockies. The staff members were kind and answered all of our questions. Dad's potential room was neither too large nor too small. The facility offered daily activities, and it was two miles from our house and five or six miles from Timmy and Linda's.

Our decision to move Dad to that facility, called Fox Hill, was made a bit easier by our kids' enthusiasm for the place. There were puzzles and games for the residents, and all three of our kids loved to visit and play with Dad there. They especially loved the ever-present popcorn machine.

Maria did a magnificent job of moving Dad's belongings from the house in Potomac to Fox Hill. His new room looked a lot like his old room, just smaller.

But the anxiety and guilt over moving Dad to Fox Hill still roiled in me. Had we made the right decision? Was it in his best interest? Or our own? Was I loving him with the same sort of unconditional love with which he loved us—even when Bobby dragged him through the front pages of the *New York Times* and when I decided not to join the Peace Corps? His example haunted me; I wanted to believe like he did, love like he did, but I felt I was falling short of the mark.

◇

CHAPTER 30

LOVE GIVER

You learn that your parent has Alzheimer's, and you keep hearing this word: "caregiver."

I grew to hate that word. It was inaccurate, belittling, and fell far short of the job requirements. You can summon the patience to be an Alzheimer's caregiver only if you care a lot, care with all your heart and soul and guts. The practical demands are so relentless that your impulse, sometimes, is to flake out, flail, and fall apart. You have to care for that other human being on a primal level, apart from seeing them as your parent. You have to love them as God's creation, part of God's grandeur, despite it all. You have to leave your ego and your own needs at the door. You can't be a caregiver; you can't look at it that way. You will fail. You have to be a love giver. I struggled for a long time before understanding that this is the only way to succeed (if that is the word), the only way to survive.

Many years into Dad's steep decline I realized that it was his example of love giving that sustained me. The only difference was that he did it for thousands, even millions of people—people with developmental disabilities, impoverished human beings all over the planet, his grandchildren, his wife, his staff at his office. The man was full of so many cares, and yet they rarely coalesced into anxiety or anger. He remained joyful and full of love.

That type of caring, let alone loving, didn't come naturally to me. I was overwhelmed by the unpredictability of the disease. I remember, two years before he died, arriving at church one Sunday morning, late as usual. Dad was sitting in the pew we usually sat in, waiting for us with Susan, his assistant. I shuffled in with the kids, heads all bowed low in a vain attempt to go unnoticed. Jeanne went in first, the three kids next, and I plopped down next to Dad. His eyes were closed, tightly. I don't know if he was snoozing or deep in prayer, but when he realized that we had arrived, he let out a loud "Hello there! Good to see you!" The people in the surrounding pews all smiled.

The Mass went on. Dad struggled to stand up and sit down at the right times, but he succeeded nonetheless.

He blew his nose time and again—this had become one of his Alzheimer's habits, and that day it agitated me. I sat in silence, disgusted by the dirty tissues in my pocket and worried that the germs on his hands would somehow touch me and I'd get a cold. I hated the fact that I was worried about his germs, but I didn't want to get sick and didn't want the kids to get sick. It would just make my hectic life more complicated.

Halfway through the sermon, Dad put his hand on my knee. I let it sit there for a few minutes, staring at it. His fingers were short and a bit stubby, thick from arthritis but beautifully manicured. These were the fingers that had given me countless back scratches as a kid and as an adult. God, I'd always loved those back scratches and begged for them not to end.

After a few minutes, his fingers moved a bit—was he giving me a tiny rub, or was it just some twitching of his fingers, something he had no idea he was doing?

It lasted for about a minute.

Then he moved his head and looked at me. I'll never forget his eyes—they were smiling. He looked down at his hand on my knee and then looked at me.

"I love you," he said.

He put his head on my shoulder for a bit.

He lifted his head, leaving his hand there on my knee.

I looked over at him; he smiled at me again and then looked back at the priest.

◇

A few weeks later, Molly came home from school and nonchalantly handed me a piece of paper. I read what she had written on it:

I am smiley and joyful
I wonder what God looks like
I hear the waves crash on the ocean
I see a bouncing tennis ball
I want peace
I am smiley and joyful

I am smiley and joyful
I pretend I am a fish when I swim
I feel the sand on my feet
I touch my grandma's hand
I am smiley and joyful

I am smiley and joyful
I understand others' feelings
I say the truth
I hope for the best
I try my hardest
I am smiley and joyful

I couldn't stop staring at her, marveling at her wonder of God, her desire for peace, and that stunning last stanza. My daughter was a younger, female version of her grandfather! Dad was still smiley and joyful, still loving me in the best way he could—he was still loving me despite his Alzheimer's, despite old age. The keen insight in her poem made me more aware than ever of his profound commitment to me even now.

It was around this time that I finally started to put to rest all the nonsense that had always driven me. Keeping up with the Kennedys, working like my life depended on it, trying to understand the fame, power, and tragedy of this family I had been born into: I was beginning to realize how little any of it mattered. I had to become a love giver. It wasn't going to be easy, but it was the only task that mattered—for Dad, and for my own future.

◇

CHAPTER 31

A HOLY CROSS

During my first few weeks at college, I went to Mass and saw a banner hanging on one of the pillars in the church. It was a quote from the book of Micah: "This is what Yahweh asks of you, only this: to act justly, to love tenderly, and to walk humbly with your God."

Those words resonated deeply with me, especially the word "only," as if the entreaties that followed—to act justly, to love tenderly, and to walk humbly—were that easy to carry out.

My years at the College of the Holy Cross had a profound impact on me. My friends, lessons, and studies there combined into a form of moral instruction. Thinking of my time there has always made me feel so hopeful for my own children—that they might someday spend four years at such a place and leave a better person for it.

By my senior year in college, I was living with nine other guys, all of whom have remained lifelong friends. One of them, Father Bill Byrne, was one of my best friends in high school, stood at the altar for Dad's funeral Mass, and today remains one of my dearest friends. Holy Cross is also the place where I met Jeanne. When we got married, we selected that Micah passage as the Old Testament reading at our wedding.

So, in the spring of 2010, when, as I was driving home, I received a phone call from the president of Holy Cross, Father Michael McFarland, I was shocked when he asked me not only to accept an honorary degree but to deliver the commencement address as well.

I told him how honored I was but said that I didn't feel that I was worthy of either the degree or delivering the address. I noted that Peter Ueberroth (who had just successfully run the Olympics in Los Angeles) had given the address when I'd graduated. My mother had delivered the address a few years prior to Ueberroth's speech. In 2007, Chief Justice John Roberts had given the graduation address, and in 2003, Chris Matthews had. These were all towering figures, and I told Father McFarland that I didn't deserve to be in their company.

Father McFarland replied matter-of-factly, "The board and I have made the decision, and we think you are worthy of it. That is not your decision. Will you accept or not?"

I said I'd do whatever he asked me to do but I would give him some time to reconsider the invitation. He said he did not need more time and asked again if I would accept. I said yes.

After hanging up, I pulled my car onto the side of the road and sat there, stunned, for a good five minutes. They were asking me to do something people would normally ask Dad to do! I wasn't worthy; I knew it. These speeches are usually given by people with worldly accomplishments or acclaim, and I was no Dad. But it troubled me even more when I tried to assess how I compared to Dad as a human being on the day-to-day level.

As one day turned into the next, I became more and

more concerned about the invitation; I assumed it had a lot
to do with my mother's and Uncle Teddy's deaths (Teddy
had died two weeks after Mom), my father's battle with
Alzheimer's, and what they and my immediate Shriver and
extended Kennedy family meant to New England. Was that
the only reason I was getting the award? Why would they
pick me, a vice president of a nonprofit? Surely they would
want a more prestigious graduation speaker.

I talked at length with Jeanne about calling Father McFarland back and turning down the offer. I was convinced
that they needed someone more prominent to elevate the
college.

Early one evening, Jeanne and I went to a fund-raiser for
a group that runs medical clinics in Haiti. I didn't want to
go; I was tired and things at work were hectic, but Jeanne
cajoled me into going. When we got there, I didn't know a
soul, which put me in an even fouler mood. Jeanne and I were
standing in the corner when one of the hosts came over to
say hello.

Soon thereafter, a short, nondescript gentleman wandered over to us to greet the cohost. He introduced himself
as Dr. Thomas Flynn, and we learned that he was one of
the founders of the group. We chatted some more; he told
us he was a pediatrician. Jeanne told him that her dad had
been a pediatrician, too. They quickly played the name
game and realized that Dr. Flynn had graduated from Holy
Cross a year ahead of Jeanne's uncle.

Afterward, Jeanne and I went out to dinner and talked
about Dr. Flynn and his work, and then the subject of my
impending speech came up again. Jeanne mentioned her
favorite graduation address ever: Dad's "break the mirrors"
speech back in 1994 at Yale. I looked at her and realized that
all I had to do was follow Dad's advice and break my mirror.

Here I was worried about my worthiness as a graduation speaker when all I really needed to do was to stop focusing on myself and focus instead on Holy Cross alumni like Dr. Flynn, who would most likely never get the chance to receive an honorary degree, and who represented everything the college taught was important.

◇

In the hotel room on the morning of the speech, as I stood in front of the mirror tightening my tie, I broke Dad's rule and gave in for a moment to the mirror. I envisioned myself walking across the stage in my robe, accepting the honorary degree, and hearing the applause at the end of my address.

But the mirror Dad had referred to, I realized, was no cheap, ordinary hotel mirror. It was the mirror of self-involvement that Dad had urged those Yale students to shatter.

I turned away from my reflection and asked Jeanne to straighten my tie. Just like during the trip home from Molly's soccer match, I felt like Dad's grace and love were showering down on me. I felt a newfound confidence; I didn't have to go up there on that stage and be a Kennedy hotshot. I had to go up there and, as Dad had said about his disease in that lucid moment a few years earlier, do the best I could with what God has given me.

As the event began, I remembered my own Holy Cross graduation, in 1986. I'd watched Dad walk across the stage then to receive an honorary degree. He'd hugged me on the stage when I'd passed him later, my own diploma in hand.

In front of the 2010 graduates, about to begin my address, I smiled at his spirit. I was at my alma mater, with my hero

giving me the faith in myself to speak in a way that honored
his example:

> By asking me to stand in front of you—a man who is not
> a high-ranking legal or political potentate, who is not a
> business tycoon or a best-selling author—by inviting me
> to speak—someone who is striving to be a pencil in God's
> hand—Holy Cross has taught me—and, I hope, all of
> you—that what is truly important in life is to accept Jesus's
> invitation to serve each other.
>
> There is an old saying in my family, made popular
> by President Kennedy, a passage from Luke: "to whom
> much is given, much is required," which speaks of obli-
> gation.
>
> I much prefer Saint Francis's invitation: "It is in giving
> that we receive."
>
> Giving brings lessons in love, compassion, humility,
> resilience, and joy that aren't available in any schoolbook,
> even those here at Holy Cross.
>
> I challenge each of you to accept the invitation to be
> a "woman for others" or a "man for others" in the Jesuit
> tradition, throughout your lives.
>
> When you accept that invitation, you might be
> ridiculed or ostracized, you surely won't have the
> biggest bank account or the biggest house, but you will
> be fulfilling the words of Dr. Martin Luther King Jr.
> when he said, "Everybody can be great because any-
> body can serve. You don't have to have a college degree
> to serve. You don't have to make your subject and your
> verb agree to serve. . . . You don't have to know the
> second theory of thermodynamics in physics to serve.
> You only need a heart full of grace. A soul generated by
> love."

As I repeated Dr. King's words, I took my eyes off the graduates and felt Dad beside me. "A heart full of grace. A soul generated by love." I felt like I was finally, albeit momentarily, close to being the man he'd always known I could be.

◇

CHAPTER 32

WHITE MASS

In September 2010, Donald Cardinal Wuerl, the archbishop of Washington, presided over the first ever "White Mass" at St. Matthew's Cathedral in Washington, D.C., in honor of people with disabilities and their caregivers. After my mother passed away, Father Bill Byrne and another friend, Father John Enzler, had proposed the concept of this special Mass to the cardinal, who'd readily agreed, hoping it would not only become a tradition in Washington but spread throughout the country.

The Mass coincided with the first ever Eunice Kennedy Shriver Challenge, a bike ride benefiting Special Olympics and Best Buddies. On Friday night, Vice President and Mrs. Biden hosted a reception at their residence in honor of the bike ride. Timmy and Anthony made remarks, and Mrs. Biden spoke eloquently about Mom's work. Vice President Biden had not been scheduled to attend, but after a change in plans, he appeared at the last moment, and he, too, praised Mom's lifelong commitment to people with developmental disabilities.

The next day, we all arose in the dark and drove down to the Washington Monument, where the bike ride commenced. It was a gorgeous, crisp fall morning. The sun was rising, and thousands of people were getting ready for the race. Jeanne, Tommy, and I rode bikes, with Emma on the back of my bike in a baby seat. Molly ran in the kids' 3K race. I had never ridden in a twenty-four-mile race before. The route took us from the Capitol to Hains Point, then along Canal Road. When we looped around to follow Canal Road back into the city for the home stretch, I saw the sun shining on the Kennedy Center, and I missed Mom terribly and longed to see Dad, who was in his apartment. But in that moment of longing, I was also incredibly proud of Mom. We were raising money for a cause she had spent her entire life fighting for, and I knew that in celebrating her we were celebrating their marriage as well. I was less enthusiastic on Sunday morning, when my hamstrings cramped up and I could barely walk, but I knew the White Mass would be the perfect way to cap the weekend.

That morning, we all gathered at St. Matthew's Cathedral. Much to my surprise, the place was jam-packed. Before the celebration began, Anthony, Alina, and their family; Jeanne, Molly, Tommy, Emma, and I; and Timmy, Linda, and their family gathered with Dad in the front row. It almost felt like a Mass for the family, especially since my old friend Father Bill Byrne was there. Cardinal Wuerl gave a terrific homily about the importance of recognizing all of God's children's gifts. He explained that the idea of calling the celebration a White Mass was because each child, when baptized, is clothed in a white garment, representing God's pure love. It is only over time that society stigmatizes that child as disabled. He wanted all of us to remember that God's love is as pure as the color white and never changes.

It was an amazing scene inside St. Matthew's: people in wheelchairs, people who were blind, people who were deaf, people with developmental disabilities, people with physical disabilities, black people, white people, people of all colors. And there was Dad in the front row, suffering from Alzheimer's, three and a half months before he was going to die, leading all of us. When he was supposed to stand, he stood; when he was supposed to kneel, he knelt; when he was supposed to bless himself, he did. And as I had seen him do so many times before, he literally mimicked the celebrant's movements, so that when the cardinal raised the chalice, Dad raised an imaginary chalice as well; when the cardinal raised the Eucharist, Dad raised an imaginary Eucharist; when the cardinal bowed his head, so did Dad; when the cardinal sang, so, too, did Dad sing.

After Mass was over, Jeanne, the kids, and I walked with Dad to a reception held in an office in the cathedral. It was filled with people using walkers and wheelchairs; there were Special Olympics athletes, deaf people signing conversations, and Seeing-Eye dogs. Dad sat in the corner, and Jeanne brought him a small plate of sandwiches, cookies, and cake. He looked absolutely ecstatic. He ate the goodies and smiled.

I wandered away for a minute to speak with Father Byrne; before too long, I turned back to see if Dad was okay. He was fine, but out of the corner of my eye, I noticed a man heading over to him. The gentleman extended his hand to Dad; Dad shook it and gave him a big smile. I could see that Dad had chocolate smudged on his lips and chin. *Oh well,* I thought. They had a short conversation, and then Dad kissed the man's hand. As the man turned away, he spotted me and walked over. "What an amazing man your father is," he said. "I have admired him for years and years. I can't believe he told me he loved me and asked God to bless me." He wiped a tear from his eye, smiled, and walked away.

CHAPTER 33

LOVE YOU WITH
A CHILD'S LOVE

At about eight-thirty one night a few weeks before Dad died, as Jeanne and I were trying to put Emma to bed and get Molly and Tommy settled down, my cell phone rang.

It was Dad's doctor, Roy Fried, calling to tell me that he had just gotten off the phone with the nurse on duty at Fox Hill. Dad's vital signs all indicated that he was having a heart attack.

I needed to make an immediate decision: call an ambulance and rush him to the hospital or leave him in his apartment and make him as comfortable as possible?

I was stunned. After thinking about it for five seconds, I asked, "Do I really have to make this decision immediately? Do I have two minutes, really? Or do I have, like, fifteen minutes or so to round up my siblings and get everyone to weigh in? Honestly, Doctor, what is my time frame?"

Dr. Fried told me that time was of the essence, though if I could get back in touch with him within ten minutes, that would be fine—but I had to hustle. He hung up.

I was frozen.

How the hell was I going to pull together a call with my four siblings, who were scattered across America and maybe even the world, in five minutes?

I immediately called my assistant, Betsy, and asked her to get a call-in line and e-mail the number to my siblings.

We were all on the phone with Dr. Fried within ten minutes.

Dealing with doctors and the science of medicine has never been my strength. I've always wanted to find a great doctor and trust him or her to do what's best, but I've learned that every doctor is pulled in countless different directions. If you are the primary caregiver for your parent or parents, you have to ask questions and keep pushing and pushing. You can never assume that the doctors and nurses involved in your parent's care are all speaking to one another because, in many cases, they are not communicating well or even communicating at all. If someone recommends a certain pill, you have to make sure that there are no side effects that will affect your parent—and you can't assume that the doctor knows what medicines your mom or dad is already taking.

Thank God that my four siblings helped, and that Timmy lived nearby. Over the last year of Dad's life, I honestly think I failed to push and probe on his medical care as much as I should have because I was so burned out. Timmy remained relentless.

The only thing I knew that night was that my dad was having a heart attack and I had minutes to make a decision about how he was to be treated.

Of course, we should have had a plan in place to deal with such a crisis. Dr. Fried had told me that the first time I'd spoken to him. He had suggested that we enroll Dad in hospice at the outset, but hospice to me meant end of life, and I didn't want to deal with that. Indeed, when the suggestion was first made, Dad had over nineteen months left to live.

The questions concerning end-of-life care were complicated by the fact that I wasn't Dad's legal proxy, so even though I was in charge of his medical care, the decision wasn't technically mine to make.

So here we were. Five adult siblings and a doctor on an emergency call at eight-forty at night, with Dad's life at stake.

Much to our amazement, Dr. Fried started the call by saying that he just heard from the nurse on duty and Dad's vital signs were moving in the right direction. It appeared, after all, that he was not having a heart attack.

"What is going on then?" Timmy asked.

Dr. Fried couldn't rule out a mild heart attack, but he also couldn't rule out bad gas or some other minor ailment.

The crisis, though, was over. We didn't have to make a decision about whether to rush him to the hospital or leave him to die in his apartment. But, again, Dr. Fried suggested that to avoid such a crisis in the future, a plan needed to be made. Again he recommended that we arrange hospice care immediately, so that Dad could die a peaceful, or at least a painless, death.

I said I would arrange a call a few days later to discuss the issue, but that now I was headed over to Dad's apartment to check on him.

When I made it to his room, he didn't even notice I was there; he was curled up in a ball, like a child. But the covers were tangled, so I smoothed them out. I looked at him and was scared out of my mind. Twenty minutes earlier I'd thought he was going to die. I used to punch him in the chest all the time and laughingly tell him, "You're going to drive me crazy until you are a hundred years old, old man—then you will die!" He would laugh, and so would I.

Could this really be happening? Was he really going to die?

I climbed into bed with him. I nudged him over a little bit to make room, and I just held him. Eventually my breathing slowed to the pace of his breathing, and we were close to being one.

But a devastating recollection disrupted the grace. I remembered a time back during my 2002 congressional race when I was tucking my son, Tommy, into bed after I'd come home late from a night of campaigning. All I could think about was the fund-raising events the next day. Here was this precious child of mine asleep but still reaching out for my love, and I was rehearsing conversations with donors!

It was the cheapest moment I'd ever lived. I knew it right after I did it, the second I walked from his bedroom into mine.

I wasn't going to blow this opportunity. I just lay there with Dad, not doing or thinking anything. Just being there. After ten minutes or so, I poked him a few times and said his name over and over. Finally, he roused himself a bit and looked up at me.

"I'm leaving now, Dad," I said. "I'll come back to visit you soon."

He opened his eyes wider and looked at me as if we had just had an hour-long chat about current events.

"I certainly hope so," he said, and smiled. "I love you."

"I love you, too," I said.

I went home. Tommy was older now, and as he walked into his room to go to bed, I smiled at him, with possibly the most loving smile I'd ever given. He smiled back and said what he says every night: "Good night, sweet dreams, sleep tight, I love you." As I heard him close his door, I smiled again, realizing how Dad must have felt all those times each and every day he smiled that gorgeous smile at all the people and things in his line of sight.

PART III

PART III

CHAPTER 34

THE LONG GOOD-BYE

Dad's appointment with his final day on his beloved earth was just about as precise as the prognostication of a baby's delivery date. We thought he was going to die on Sunday, then Monday, but on Tuesday morning, the doctor said Dad had stabilized and could live for a few days more. We were at the hospital and didn't know what to do. Some of the family from California started making plans to fly home; the grandkids who were in college in the Northeast started booking train reservations. Jeanne and I headed home with our kids and had a hesitant lunch with Anthony, Alina, and their family.

At about three P.M., my sister-in-law Linda called: "Your dad is fading really fast. Hurry over here—it may already be too late."

We bolted out the door and drove like lunatics to Suburban Hospital, four miles away.

Anthony and I burst into the hospital room, and Linda and Courtney Kennedy gave us kisses and left.

Dad had died in front of them moments prior.

Bobby, Maria, and Timmy arrived about five minutes later.

I called our local parish priest, Bill English, and asked him to come over.

We started to say the Rosary while we waited for him—twenty-nine of us jammed into Dad's hospital room. Father English arrived and led us in prayer. He then asked if anyone wanted to offer some thoughts. Timmy said a prayer of thanksgiving for Dad; others offered reminiscences, each unique to that person's experience with Dad, each heartfelt and beautiful.

I said, "I would like to offer a prayer of thanks for all the nurses and doctors and caretakers who have helped Dad over the years, especially for Rags, his great friend. We pray to the Lord."

And then Anthony blew us all away.

We'd all had a great relationship with Mom, though Anthony had had a particularly intense one. He was the youngest; he looked a lot like Mom's oldest brother, Joe; and it was clear that Mom had had a huge crush on Joe growing up. Although Anthony gets credited with starting Best Buddies and growing it all over the world, he himself says Mom was his closest partner and confidante in building the organization.

"I hope that every girl in this room finds a man who respects and loves her every day in every way like Dad loved and respected and took care of Mom," he said. It was the shortest prayer of all of them, but the one that seemed most perfect to me.

Together we all said, "Lord, hear our prayer."

After a few minutes, family members started to stagger out of the room. Each person stopped to take one long, last look at Dad, and most then turned one last time again, as if hoping still that this was a mirage.

I faced my siblings and asked whether I should call the two funeral directors, John and Terry McHugh, who were waiting outside the hospital. I had phoned them about an hour earlier and told them to wait out front until I called again. We all agreed that it was time.

I knew that once I called, they would be there quickly, but I still found their very presence jarring—two young men, in suits, with somber looks on their faces. I was relieved to see two professionals there to help—but also repulsed by them. They were going to take Dad away from me, right? Who the hell were these guys to do such a thing?

I walked them into Dad's hospital room. John told me that he and Terry had everything under control and that I could leave now.

But I said that I wanted to be there, to help move Dad onto the gurney they had brought and to accompany him to the hearse. John agreed. We started the process of getting Dad prepared to leave, making sure that he was free and clear of needles and tubes. We lifted him from his bed and slid him into a body bag. I watched as John zipped the bag closed.

Then the three of us wheeled him to the elevator. John suggested that we take the back elevator so that the press that had gathered out front wouldn't see Dad being put into the hearse. As we wheeled the gurney down the hallway toward the back elevator, I suddenly saw the gurney itself as the enemy, as a malevolent force that was insistently carrying Dad away from me.

We finally arrived at the elevator and pushed the Down button. I wanted to drag the gurney back, resist, make one last stand against this impossibility.

The elevator doors opened, and John and Terry pushed the gurney inside. The wheels made a jarring sound as they crossed the steel threshold of the elevator.

John turned to me and said, "We have it covered from here, Mark. Go home and be with your family."

I stared blankly at him, then looked down at that goddamn

gurney again. That was what I called it in my head. In his final years, Dad, so devout a man, had taken to saying "god-damn it" often. But it wasn't a curse; it was a superlative, a term of endearment. "I love you, goddamn it!" he would say at times. It was as if he knew God had a sense of humor, and with a bit of a devil-may-care epithet, he was making that humorous God complicit in his declarations of love.

In my head, I used it in the vulgar sense. I felt angry—angry that I hadn't been there when he died, angry that he was gone, angry at the damn gurney that was so determined to have its way with his body. Angry at God.

I stepped into the elevator, too.

I stuttered, "Are you sure?"

They both nodded. They were doing their job well—they were standing firm, almost giving me orders. I relented.

I turned and walked out of the elevator, then turned back. The two of them flanked my dad, one on each side. John said, "We will take care of him. Don't worry. Your dad was a good man."

I looked at them. The elevator doors shut. I stared at the closed door. Numb.

I heard that phrase, "a good man," repeating itself in my head. The accumulation of the use of this tag, this epitaph, would make it the defining description of Dad for me over the coming weeks. But the first time was the sweetest. It wasn't too much; it wasn't too little. John, with his boyish looks and steady voice, had said the words that enabled me to allow the doors to close on Dad's life on earth.

◇

CHAPTER 35

A BEAUTIFUL DAY

The day of the wake, Dad was the calmest, as usual. My head was spinning. Jeanne and I had put up a tent in our backyard and were expecting hundreds of people to stop in after the service. The caterers were busy setting up; the doorbell kept ringing. The Montgomery County government had offered a police escort for the drive into D.C. for the wake, and the officers had arrived an hour earlier than expected.

Dad was at rest in his coffin in our living room, the same place he had been since we'd brought him back from the funeral parlor. It was an open coffin, and he looked so content. I know that it is a bit unusual nowadays to have a loved one's body in your home, but the five of us never considered anything else. When Mom and Dad died, we thought it best to have visiting hours at one of their favorite local churches, but we wanted them at home during the days of preparing and waiting for the funeral. Both of them had spent most of their adult lives creating a space, a place, that provided security, warmth, support, and, most importantly, love for us kids. We felt that they should pass their last few days on earth in such a place.

Jeanne and I discussed whether having Dad in our home

would negatively affect our children. Would they have nightmares or be upset?

Dad had always taught us that death is part of life. "It's not something to deny," he'd say, "it's to be embraced." So we'd brought him home to our house.

Our good friend Rob Granader told me months after the funeral: "I walked into your home and the woman who answered the front door said, 'Please go say hello to Grandpa.' I walked into the next room, and there was Sarge. I was by myself and had never experienced anything like that before. About five minutes later, Jeanne walked in the front door with Emma. She gave me a big hug and told Emma to go say good night to Grandpa. Emma ran toward the coffin as if her granddad was sitting there in a chair and she was going to jump into his lap. She knelt down and said a prayer and then said, 'I love you, Grandpa.' She turned and waved to Jeanne and me, said good night, and ran up the stairs. It was as if your dad was still a part of your family even after death."

It felt good and right to have Dad in our house for those few days. Every time I walked by him, I smiled and asked for a little of his grace and peace; he'd always had it in life, and he certainly had it now, in death.

The public service at Holy Trinity Catholic Church was a great way to begin Dad's Irish wake. The tributes—from Maryland congressman Steny Hoyer; Dad's Peace Corps colleague C. Payne Lucas; former Peace Corps volunteer Maureen Orth; former Peace Corps volunteer Senator Chris Dodd; Colman McCarthy, Dad's colleague in the War on Poverty; Dad's longtime colleague Bill Moyers; and former senator George McGovern—were thoughtful and funny. They made us laugh and cry, and laugh and cry all over again.

When I looked at Colman, I remembered how he ended up living in Washington, D.C.: in the summer of 1966, just a few months removed from five years in a Trappist monastery,

Colman was a freelance writer penning pieces about the civil rights movement. He sold an article to the *National Catholic Reporter* criticizing one of Dad's anti-poverty programs. Dad read it, called him up, and invited him to come to D.C. to interview for a job. Dad told Colman that he could use a "no-man because I already have enough yes-men."

Over a four-hour dinner, they discussed Thomas Merton, Flannery O'Connor, Leon Bloy, and others. They didn't discuss politics at all. At the end of the night, Dad offered Colman a job.

After working for Dad for three years, Colman went on to be a nationally syndicated columnist for the *Washington Post*.

I chuckled to myself as I thought about that dinner. *Dad really had an eye for talent, didn't he?* I thought. I remembered hearing Scott Stossel, his biographer, sitting on a panel with Tim Russert, Maureen Orth, Tom Friedman, Congressman Harold Ford, and World Bank president James Wolfensohn. They had gathered to discuss the release of Scott's biography, *Sarge*. When it came time for Scott to speak, he mentioned each of his fellow panelists by name and then paused and said, "All of these people and me on a panel—one of us is not like the others!"

The audience roared. Scott then said, "Actually, I think I'm here not just as Mr. Shriver's biographer but I am emblematic of the way Mr. Shriver operated—he reached out and found people all over this country, and all over the world, who he thought had special talent. Many of us couldn't even see it in ourselves but Mr. Shriver could. And he gave people like me a chance to make a difference."

Scott is now editor of *The Atlantic*.

The most poignant moment was when eighty-nine-year-old George McGovern walked slowly to the altar and spoke. "Sargent Shriver was the kindest, the most cheerful, the

most optimistic person I've met in fifty years of public life,"
he said. "It's remarkable that those virtues could all be combined in one personality. I don't ever recall him being down
in the dumps. He must have had days like that, but nobody
ever saw them if he did."

And then he recalled the words Dad had said to him
shortly after they'd suffered that landside defeat, losing even
McGovern's home state of South Dakota. McGovern's wife,
Eleanor, was crying when Dad "put an arm around me and
around Eleanor, and he said, 'You know, George, we lost
forty-nine states but we never lost our souls.'"

After the two-hour service, we drove back to our house
for the afterparty. The Irish singer and Academy Award win-
ner Glen Hansard sang songs in the living room as Dad lay
listening peacefully. We ate good food together and raised
many a toast to Dad.

We finally shut the party down at twelve-thirty A.M. A
great Irish wake indeed.

But I didn't sleep well and got up at four. I tiptoed past
my kids' rooms and headed downstairs. I had my eulogy in
hand, the one I had started to write on that plane ride to Los
Angeles. I liked it, but the intervening days had made clear
to me that it was not what it should be. I needed to read it
aloud to the best editor I've ever had.

It was pitch-black, except for two flickering candles, one
at each end of the coffin. I knelt down, spread the eulogy on
the closed side of the coffin, and started to read aloud to Dad.

The word "eulogy," I'd learned earlier that week, means
"good words" in the original Greek. Great men and women
were coming to the funeral to speak: former president Clinton and Vice President Biden would speak; Bono, Wyclef
Jean, Vanessa Williams, and Glen would sing; and Donald
Cardinal Wuerl, Archbishop of Washington, would preside
and give the homily.

But the constant comments about "a good man," not the great men and women who would share the lectern with me, were what had upped the ante. The great men and women would cover the great words, but I needed good words, holy words, to memorialize a "good man." That was, paradoxically, harder.

As I knelt there in front of him, I thought how much Dad would have loved being at the party. He was, as so many witnesses attested, so much fun to be around. His rich and rigid interior life in no way got in the way of his incessant quest for joy—whether nursing a vodka and tonic with my college friends, playing catch with his grandkids, or cheering on Special Olympic athletes at the finish line. He was joyful at his very core.

I knew that my eulogy fell short—it had captured his accomplishments as a public servant and father, but it hadn't fully done justice to his rollicking spirit, to his joy. I had been trying to come up with the right words, the so-called great words a eulogy requires, but I realized I had to scale it back and focus simply on Dad's goodness. So I picked up my text and started to revise it on top of Dad's coffin.

At first, nothing happened. I didn't change a word. I just kept reading the eulogy—I knew it wasn't altogether right, but I couldn't find the words that would make it better.

Then, slowly, I started to hear Dad's voice; I started to imagine his smile, his bounce, his insistent hopefulness.

I changed a word here and a few words there.

I sat in silence some more. *I need help,* I thought. *I need a lot of help.* I listened for some sign.

And again, slowly, I saw Dad smile, heard him give advice, saw him in our church, holding my hand, praying.

I changed a few more words.

Then I rewrote a paragraph.

I knew I needed to say something like this: he was good

to everyone equally; he was a good man in his personal life
and in his civic life, not just in Washington power circles or
at Kennedy compound gatherings but in the more difficult
and mundane endeavors and interactions that fill our days.

So I wrote and scratched things out and looked to Dad
for encouragement as I came up with, of all things, a polite
and slight correction to his comment that day years ago as
we looked into the sunrise at the end of the Chesapeake Bay
Bridge:

> I think Dad had it ever so slightly wrong. He didn't have
> to die to meet God and experience that beauty. Dad truly
> saw the beauty of that sunrise in each of us. His bound-
> less energy was focused on creating a heaven right here
> on earth, on creating moments of beauty—like that
> sunrise—that all of us can share. He knew he couldn't do
> it alone—that's why he went to Mass every day, to ask for
> help, guidance, and support.

I made some more adjustments, then put my pen down.
We had nailed it, he and I. My revised eulogy was now good
enough not just for the crowd and his church, the cardinal
and the First Lady, the vice president and the former president, or even for those who might watch it on TV—no, it was
now good enough for the greatest good man I ever knew.

I looked up and noticed that the sun was rising. In a
couple of hours, everyone would gather at our house and
prepare to go to the church for the funeral Mass. I could
hear Jeanne moving around upstairs and Emma's little feet
running along the hallway. The day itself felt like it was
moving us forward with it.

I started visualizing what was to come: the Mass itself; the
cardinal at the altar; the singing of the songs; my kids, nieces,
and nephews crying one second and laughing the next.

I knew that Dad had loved music, but he'd tended to listen to opera and classical records. Often when I would walk into their home, I'd hear the stereo system blasting Bach or Beethoven while Dad sat in the living room, reading. I decided to follow his lead—I went over to our stereo and put on my favorite song, "Beautiful Day" by U2. As it started to play, I sat in a chair by the coffin and read the eulogy one more time. The music took over. "It's a beautiful day. Don't let it get away—it's a beautiful day."

After the song finished, I went back to the stereo and hit Replay, this time turning it up a bit louder. I did not sit down to read, but instead stood there looking at my dad in his coffin and sang the song out loud.

I decided to play the song once more, this time even louder. I cranked it up and sang: "What you don't have, you don't need it now / What you don't know, you can feel it somehow / What you don't have, you don't need it now, don't need it now / It was a beautiful day."

Three times was the charm. I felt great—we were celebrating Dad's life. We were celebrating his love affair with God. We were celebrating the fact that he was finally meeting the Creator he'd so longed to meet, and we were celebrating his longed-for reunion with my mother.

I rushed back into the text of my eulogy, and where I had written the phrase "a good day," in a couple of places, I changed it to "a beautiful day."

Then I went upstairs and prepared for everyone's arrival. Friends dropped off coffee and doughnuts, and family members started arriving. Just before it was time to leave for the funeral, the entire family—all five children, all nineteen grandchildren, and all five in-laws—came together in the living room to say some last prayers. We gathered in a big circle and held hands and said an Our Father and a Hail Mary.

After the prayers, Timmy said a few words about how he was feeling, and a few others offered their thoughts as well. I spoke last and said: "I know that today will be painful and sad but, ultimately, every day with Dad has been a gift, and every day he spent with us he treasured, not only the day, but also the moment. I hope we treasure the funeral and the beauty of Dad being with God. It's gonna be a beautiful day."

◇

CHAPTER 36

SHOCK ME WITH YOUR LOVE

The funeral Mass was at Our Lady of Mercy, Dad's home parish, where he'd attended daily Mass most mornings. Walking into the church, I was struck by a feeling of déjà vu. *Didn't we just do the exact same thing about a day ago?* I thought. *Weren't we just in Hyannis Port burying Mom?*

The main actors were different; Cardinal Wuerl, Father English, and my old friend Father Bill Byrne were leading this funeral, whereas Father Richard Fragomeni had led the funeral in Hyannis Port. But the coffin, the pallbearers, the vestibule filled with people with long faces nodding at me—all of that felt the same.

The cardinal said the opening prayer, the music started, and the pallbearers progressed into the church. It did feel the same but, indeed, it was different from Hyannis Port in August just seventeen months earlier. That day had been hot, really hot. We'd carried Mom's coffin about four blocks to the church, sweating in our suits the whole way, while in Dad's case, the hearse carried the coffin to the front of the church and we carried him in from there.

And the coffin was different. He had asked for the Trappist burlap sack; I'd chosen the simplest Trappist coffin available. But I looked at it as we walked into the church, and my heart sank. There was President Clinton, Vice President Biden, Mrs. Obama, countless members of Congress, Cabinet secretaries, Bono, Oprah, and friends everywhere.

What would they think when they saw that plain walnut box? When they found out that I had chosen the coffin, would they think, *What a cheap bastard, putting his ninety-five-year-old father, a great American, in the cheapest plain box imaginable*?

The pallbearer situation was the same as at Mom's service: there were too many of us, and we were literally tripping over ourselves as we walked down the aisle. Our usual madhouse. When we carried Mom into the church, we were jammed together, and Tommy was so close to me that I moved outside of him to let him keep his grip. The center aisle of St. Francis Xavier Church in Hyannis Port is so narrow that my thigh banged into every pew. The black-and-blue marks stayed with me for weeks.

In this case, there was plenty of space and no bruises, but we still had to take a lot of short, choppy steps. We rested the coffin at the foot of the altar and filed into the front pew. I was at the end, farthest from the coffin, which was in the center of the church. I looked to my right and again saw that plain coffin, now draped with a beautiful white burial cloth. I stared at it, stunned, still, that Dad was in there, that the church was jammed, nervous that I had to speak, nervous that the funeral was being televised. I lifted my eyes from the coffin and saw the first pew: Mrs. Obama, Biden, Clinton. What were they thinking looking at that coffin: What a great man he was? What a cheap coffin that is?

Then I glanced away, looking first at Father Byrne, on the altar, and then at Molly and Tommy, who were altar servers.

My gaze lingered on Tommy. *Three generations of Shriver males gathered together,* I thought. The last time that will happen—at least until I'm an old grandpa myself. *What will*

he look like when I become a grandfather? Will I be as good a grand-
father to his kids as Dad was to mine? Then the similarities
between Tommy and Dad walloped me.

After Mom died and we prayed at the Cape house, when
we said the Rosary, Timmy always led. When he finished
the first decade, he would ask, "Who wants to lead the next
decade?" There would, inevitably, be silence and a lot of
downcast heads. Then we'd all hear a soft voice speak out
with a bit of a lisp: "I will, Uncle Timmy." And bang, nine-
year-old Tommy would lead. He knew the prayers inside
and out. He knew them because the school he attends,
Mater Dei (the name means "Mother of God" in Latin), is
old-school. And I mean old-school.

The teachers drill prayers into the heads of each and every
student. Those boys memorize prayers, memorize how to say
the Rosary, memorize the exact same information Dad himself memorized as a child. They use pen and paper—no com-
puters. They have recess and sports: the teachers send the boys
outside, make them run around and organize their own games.
When there are disagreements, the boys have to work them
out among themselves. The school motto is simple: "Work
hard, play hard, pray hard, but most of all, be a good guy."

I looked at that boy with his grandpa's faith and confident reliance on the articles of that faith, and I realized that
Tommy was living that motto well, just like Dad had.

I smiled. The pressure was off. I looked at that coffin; the
choice now made eminent sense. Yes, Dad had had wealth,
he had traveled the world, but ultimately, he had wanted to
keep his life simple—to focus on what was really important
and what God asked him to do. He played hard, prayed
hard, but most of all, he lived trying to be not just a good
guy but a good guy focused on others. In death, he'd wanted
to keep it simple, too, so he'd chosen the simplest way to be
buried.

He was leading me, instructing me; he was showing me even as he lay in his coffin at his last Mass. The coffin was a statement about his faith. The Peace Corps, Head Start, Legal Services, and Special Olympics were all ways to express faith in action, and so, too, was that coffin a sign of his faith and hope and love.

As I sat in the pew at his funeral, his words came back to me again: "I'm doing the best I can with what God has given me." Out of all his great words throughout the years, these were the ones sustaining me that day, telling me, Do the best you can with it, boy, and I'll be proud simply of that.

Anthony got up to welcome everyone before the opening prayer.

Smiling mischievously, he said:

> To be honest with you, I think some time's going to go by and people are going to debate what my father's greatest accomplishments have been over his career—whether it's Head Start or the Job Corps or VISTA or Foster Grandparents or the Peace Corps. But for me his greatest accomplishment, as his son, will always be having produced this at the age of fifty.

When Anthony said "having produced this," he pointed at himself! Indeed, Dad had become a father for the fifth time at the age of fifty. The place roared—the funeral was taking on the air of a celebration.

The cardinal began the Mass in tune—he played along with Anthony's prediction that everyone would talk for too long by saying that no one had yet put a time limit on his homilies and he was happy about that!

As the Mass proceeded, I paid close attention to Father Byrne and Dad's parish priest, Father English. One was a dear old friend, and the other had been a source of thought-

ful insight over our four years of friendship. There were fifteen other priests there, filling a couple of pews—an odd
assortment from all parts of Dad's life. I thought for a moment
of the photos of Dad as an altar boy, and the ones of Cardinal Gibbons at his home. He would have loved a photo of
this one, too.

The Mass progressed. Wyclef Jean sang the first respon-
sorial psalm, Psalm 98, in reggae style; Vanessa Williams sang
"Soon and Very Soon"; and Bono and Glen Hansard sang
"Make Me a Channel of Your Peace."

When it came time for my siblings and me to speak,
we rose together and walked to the lectern. Anthony had
extended the welcome, so he stayed in his pew. Maria went
first; Timmy, Bobby, and I stood behind her. As I listened to
my sister and brothers speak, I found myself continually
looking at the back wall of the Church with the Stations of
the Cross stretched across it.

And that's when I had an epiphany, the sort of sudden,
and often jarring, realization about your life and deeds that I
first learned about back in high school when we read James
Joyce's short story "The Dead." At the end of the story, the
main character, Gabriel, watches his wife sleeping as the snow
falls outside a window. Events that evening had triggered a
startling revelation in him about his life and wife, his past
and probably his future. It's a classic story, and it ends with
one of the great moments of self-discovery—for better or
worse—in literature.

Well, mine was this: I saw the Stations of the Cross on
the back wall of the church—only instead of Jesus being
whipped and crowned with thorns, instead of Jesus assum-
ing the weight of the cross, instead of Jesus falling down and
being helped up by Simon and having his face wiped by
Veronica, I saw Dad in all his Alzheimer's agony. We Catholics call the last few days of Christ's life the Passion. I'd

always found the word choice odd. I usually thought of passion as a good thing—in work, in marriage, in friendship. But in Jesus's case, it referred to the unimaginably hard final days.

I want to be clear: in no way am I confusing or conflating Jesus and Dad. But, yes, I am confusing and conflating them to the extent that it is possible, if not helpful, to confuse every human life with the life of Christ. Jesus experienced agony: in the Garden of Gethsemane Judas betrayed him, and Jesus felt agony; three times Peter denied knowing him, and Jesus experienced agony; on the cross, he looked down at his mother at his feet and, I think, felt the greatest agony of all—seeing her suffer as she watched him suffer.

But if the agony and the very story of Jesus serve their truest purpose, we all come to identify with the death of the man who came to give us eternal life.

So as I stood there, I saw Dad and thought again about what he had said to me: "I'm doing the best I can with what God has given me." He lived passionately, got his passion from his faith, but knew, I do not doubt, that his life, like most lives, would end in trial.

And I realized that I wouldn't be surprised to hear that Jesus had said the exact same thing: "I'm doing the best I can with what God has given me."

Alzheimer's was Dad's cross—indeed, the cross for all of us who loved him. He labored with its weight, and he carried it to his certain destination. We, his children and friends, buckled under it as we tried to help him lift it; various and lovely people along the way wiped our faces, prayed for us, supported him.

And yet he knew all along, from his announcement of his disease right through those shockingly lucid moments in the midst of its onslaught, what he was up against, what he was carrying.

When my turn to speak came, I looked over at my family one last time for the burst of confidence they always give me. I was ready to do the best I could.

And I said, in part:

Dad was joyful until the day he died, and I think that joy was deeply rooted in his love affair with God. Daddy loved God, and God loved him right back. He went to daily Mass at seven or eight-thirty, usually right in the chapel over there. And I mean he went every day, regardless of where he was. I vividly remember checking into hotels all across America and around the world and always knowing the first question Daddy would ask: "Do you have a Mass schedule?"

Daddy was on his knees, acknowledging that he needed God's help and guidance every day of his life. He knew that if he gave himself to God and asked God to be in control, then it was going to be a beautiful day. Whether he was interacting with a president, vice president, First Lady, or cardinal—or whether he was talking to a cab driver, a trash collector, or a two-year-old grandchild— he thought you were sent from God to be with him that day and there was nobody more important than you at that very moment. You were God's gift to him. Daddy let go; God was in control—oh, what a relationship they had!

When he was creating the Peace Corps from scratch, many people thought he was naïve, too idealistic to want to send a bunch of young Americans abroad, have them live in the very poorest parts of the world, working side by side with the poor.

Daddy saw people helping people. He saw that deep inside us all, we all long to help each other. He saw his work, whether it was with the Chicago Board of Education, the Peace Corps, or Special Olympics, as an instrument to spread God's love. He never saw his "work" as a job that had to be done; he never punched a clock. No, he saw his efforts as a way to bring people together to help one another and, in so doing, to spread love.

He saw each of us as a creature of God's love. Every day he went to church to be renewed in that love, to say thank you for that love, to celebrate and be energized by that love—no wonder he went to work joyfully every day.

And that love permeated his core and never left him.

Alzheimer's robs you of so much. In Dad's case, it stripped him to the core and beautifully showed us who he was, and what our core should look like. . . .

For my father, this man of God, life has changed, not ended—his love affair with God has only deepened. How lucky, indeed, are the Lucky 7, as he'd always called our family? How lucky are all of us—actually, how blessed are all of us to have known such a man?

God bless you, Daddy.

After I finished, we all walked back to our seats. I felt like God was carrying me to my pew. I didn't feel my legs moving or see the crowd. I just felt, like at the Holy Cross speech, a sense of blessing. A great, big, enveloping blessing.

And I felt hopeful. This wasn't the end of Dad, merely the end of his Passion and the beginning of my new relationship with him. I'd always tried to live the way he did, but in that moment, I began to see his life less as a challenge to measure up to and more as a form of guidance to heed. I didn't have to be as good as he was at the tough stuff of faith and hope and love—all I had to do was the best I could. At first I discounted my sudden clarity; I had heard about plenty of these Saul-to-Paul moments and knew that most people went right back to their old ways soon after. But then I cut myself some slack—the previous decade of Dad's illness had been my education, my tutorial in trying to learn to live like Dad. This wasn't an epiphany; it was a culmination. The change had been taking hold all along. This was my last day in Dad's physical presence, but my first with him as my daily mentor.

CHAPTER **3 7**

◇

GRANDPA!

D ad was going to be buried next to Mom in a small cemetery on Cape Cod, and we would all head there after the funeral reception. But first, as I stood in the hallway greeting people after the funeral, I heard that golden phrase over and over again: a good man. We tried to leave the reception several times, but the family couldn't seem to cohere. We kept lingering, and people said it again and again: what a good man he was!

We finally got our act together and drove to Dulles International Airport for the charter flight to Massachusetts.

Sitting in the airplane gave everyone permission to deflate. I collapsed into the window seat of an empty row. Jeanne joined me, and we gently shooed the kids away to sit with their cousins at the back of the plane.

As the plane taxied, the conversation died down, and my mind wandered back to my eulogy. Had it been good enough? Had I forgotten a page or even two? Had I mispronounced some words?

The sun was still shining when we escaped into the sky, a brilliant winter sun that was headed west as we were headed north. It reminded me of that trip across the bay decades ago. This sun's beauty could make you believe in God.

The flight to Massachusetts was brief. I could soon see the familiar shoreline of the commonwealth, and my mind wandered to the wonderful times I had spent on the ocean with Dad.

Looking out the window, I saw a beautiful sunset. The sky was on fire. As the plane pitched, the views of the sunset shifted. The kids noticed, and we all stared out our windows and gasped. I couldn't help but feel that somehow Dad had been united with that sun and all of God's gorgeous creation he loved so much.

When we landed, the sun had almost set. It's amazing how the sun can shine for twelve hours a day but an unbelievable sunset is over in a matter of minutes. *Why is that?* I wondered.

We were met on the tarmac by a military honor guard there to honor Dad for his service in the navy. By the time the airplane door opened, the sun had set, the wind had picked up, and the cold air made me feel empty. The sunset and clouds had heartened me; now I suddenly felt alone without him.

We disembarked and waited for the coffin. The honor guard members stood straight, heedless of the wind and the chill. I knew something of the discipline required from these men and women from my college roommate Tim Royston, who had become a U.S. Marine fighter pilot. Dad had joined the navy right out of Yale Law School. He'd had that military discipline, too, and such admiration for those who served our country—surely he would have appreciated these men and women who braved the cold to show their respect for an old sailor.

Once the casket had been loaded into the hearse, I slid into the front seat to accompany Dad to his final resting place. The rest of the family boarded a bus and followed behind the police escort. It was a forty-five-minute drive, winding through the small towns of Cape Cod until we reached the cemetery in Osterville.

A handful of television cameras greeted us at the entrance to the cemetery, but there were only a few folks by the grave site, at the rear of the cemetery. Anthony had arranged for Father Mark Hession, from Our Lady of Victory, the church we attended in the summertime, to be there. Father Mark was accompanied by Beverly Donheiser, a soprano, who led us in song. A small tent had been erected over the burial site, illuminated by two spotlights.

To my amazement, we were met by another group of military pallbearers. They, too, had been waiting outside in the freezing cold, to carry Dad the twenty yards from the hearse to the grave site. I could see their breath in the frigid night air as they struggled with the coffin over the bumpy terrain, in tight quarters. We had all gathered underneath the tent, holding candles. The pallbearers placed the coffin on a rig in the center of the space. They precisely folded the American flag that draped the coffin. They handed the flag to Bobby, then gave each of us a folded flag as well. I thanked the man who handed me my flag, trying to make eye contact, but he barely nodded. He and his colleagues were so singular in their work.

Father Mark led us in some prayers and said a few words, Beverly sang two songs, a military bugler played "Taps," and that was it.

It was over.

But no one moved.

The graveyard workers, who had been hanging around outside the tent, eventually wandered over. One of the guys asked Anthony whether he wanted them to lower the coffin into the encasement. Anthony said, "Yes, we are staying here until that's done." So the workers lowered the coffin into the encasement and then lowered the encasement into the ground.

We all stood or knelt in silence, watching. It was the exact same process we had gone through just seventeen months earlier, with Mom, at the exact same spot. Her headstone stood right there alongside where Dad was being lowered.

When the encasement finally hit the bottom, there was a minute or two of silence. A flower was thrown into the hole; then some more flowers were tossed, and then some candles.

It was cold and oh so quiet.

As we pulled out of the cemetery, we changed our plans and decided to take a ten-minute detour to Hyannis Port to see the ocean and our parents' home, the house where we had spent so many joyous summer days and nights. Since the house was closed for the winter, the bus parked in the beach club parking lot, some two hundred yards from the house, so we could get out and walk to the shore.

It was an absolutely clear night, and the sky was filled with stars. The tide was very low, so all of us could walk side by side on the beach; the kids skipped stones and ran around screaming at one another. Soon people started to complain about the temperature, but before we headed back to the bus, Timmy suggested that we all hold hands and form a huge circle. We did. There was lots of giggling and yelling until Timmy said, "On the count of three, let's all run into the middle and yell, 'Grandpa!'"

So together we shouted, "One, two, three!" and ran at each other like lunatics and when we, all twenty-nine of us, arrived in the center, we yelled, "Grandpa!"

We kept shouting that title, the one he was most proud of.

◇

CHAPTER 38

PACKING UP A LIFE

Packing up a life—what an absurd activity! A coffin feels fittingly dramatic and profound; the boxes of stuff make you feel like the end of a life means little more than moving a house.

A few weeks after the funeral, I woke up determined to pack up or give away all of Dad's remaining belongings that very day.

When I entered his room at Fox Hill, I had a sense of déjà vu yet again. Hadn't I just moved him out of his bedroom? This time, the space was smaller but the task no less daunting.

Some of the pictures from the "big house" had made it to Fox Hill. The picture of him in his altar boy garb with the parish priest; the picture taken at Westminster of Cardinal Gibbons seated next to President Taft, with Dad's father standing in the background; the pictures of his mother and father; the rectangular frame with the three pictures of Mom; the picture of Mary, the mother of Jesus; and a painting of the crucifix.

This day, alone in his last room, I realized that he'd wanted his bedroom to be a sacred space with sacred images. These pictures had been in his bedroom at Timberlawn and had survived the move to the D.C. home, then to the Potomac "big house," and finally here.

The monastic simplicity of his rooms, I came to see, was what enabled him to grapple with so many complex and disparate issues during the day. He knew what he needed; it was as simple as simplicity itself.

As I sat there, I thought back to his final letter. He had written it as if he were a man in rapture; he wrote with the language of a firebrand Southern Baptist preacher; he was, as a person I knew who had found God in a maximum-security prison liked to say, "on fire for the Lord." But the shining language showed me a side of Dad that the photographs in his room made even more profound. He'd written:

> Indeed, I expect to get to eternity first. . . . I will have picked a nice place to live like Timberlawn or Avondale or the Cape. I will have reservations at the best table at the best restaurant and tickets on the aisle for the best show on the very first night you come to join me in an eternal love affair with each other, with our children, with the Blessed Mother, and with that unbelievable incandescent, white, hot, atomic furnace of love and laughter and life— the greatest host of the greatest party with the greatest guest list of all time—that perfect person, Jesus the Christ.

He was not like the typical politician who talks about God as often as he mentions his mother or wife. He was very private about it but also very rigid. Faith was a very practical, direction-giving thing for Dad.

But I never had fully grasped—until that airplane ride, the "good man" comments, the revision of my eulogy, and the sight of these sober photographs—the degree to which faith was the basis of his daily work and interaction. I fully and finally understood that he had always had one eye on the sky, if you will. In that more spiritual, almost transcendental sense, his faith helped him focus his ambition, the contagious disease infecting so many in his adopted town of Washington. His abiding ambition was to be a faithful son of God.

Despite my determination to pack everything up in one day, I had, by all external standards of productivity, wasted the day. The people at Fox Hill were extraordinarily kind and professional, but I knew I was pushing my luck. I had to finish the packing; and I had to get on with my life. I passed an administrator in the hall and promised that I was almost finished.

The next day, I focused on Dad's clothes and books. The clothes he had were mostly old, and the books were far fewer than what we had moved just sixteen months earlier.

Thumbing through them, I noticed how much underlining he'd done. He'd scribbled notes in the margins. He'd drawn arrows and so many exclamation points. I had seen such markings countless times before, but I grew enthralled and again lost track of time.

I spent that day, I realized later, in one long conversation with him. He'd been underlining and notating for me. He was communicating with me through these last few books and the monthly missalettes he'd saved. I found a copy of the *Baltimore Catechism* on the shelf in his closet. I don't know if it was Dad's, but I am sure that someone was reading it to him during his final months of life. For Dad's generation of Catholic schoolboys, that book ranked near the Bible in terms of importance. I'd always understood it as a practical guide to the Bible's spiritual lessons and demands, but I'd never paid it much heed; my generation of Catholics—post–Vatican II and fully secular—had bigger things on our minds than a practical guide to living a proper life.

I opened it and read:

Who made us? God made us.

Who is God? God is the Supreme Being, infinitely perfect, who made all things and keeps them in existence.

Why did God make us? God made us to show forth his goodness and to share with us his everlasting happiness in heaven.

What must we do to gain the happiness of heaven? To gain the happiness of heaven, we must know, love, and serve God in this world.

From whom do we learn to know, love, and serve God? We learn to know, love, and serve God from Jesus Christ, the Son of God, who teaches us through the Catholic Church.

We had picked this part of the text for Dad's funeral program. When Timmy had first suggested it, I'd agreed without much thought, but here in Dad's room, I realized we had gotten very close to the heart of him.

◇

A week or so later, I got up early and headed to our basement to begin organizing some of the many letters Dad had written to me over the years. I read a bunch of them, but they were more mundane than inspirational—a note about Pedro Martínez's most recent pitching gem and a box score from that game; an article from the Catholic magazine *Commonweal;* a copy of a letter he'd sent to a college president. Each one included underlining and plenty of exclamation points.

My eyes wandered from the files and settled on a bookcase in the corner. I noticed, for the first time in who knew how long, that I had placed a couple of scrapbooks on the bottom shelf.

I pulled one out and looked through it and smiled, a lot. When Anthony and I were in high school, Mom had gone through a stage when she started making scrapbooks. And she'd encouraged us to do the same. Clearly, Mom had made this one. There was no order to the contents: here a picture of Anthony and me playing with puppies in the backyard of Timberlawn when we were youngsters, next a picture of Aunt Rosemary, then a picture of Rags with Timmy, followed by a picture of Special Olympics athletes, then a speech by Uncle Teddy.

I had to lift the plastic off each page in order to see the photos clearly or to read the speech. And the entire speech, six pages long, was jammed under that plastic sheet!

I could tell that Mom had made the scrapbook on the fly. She'd had such an active mind and boundless energy. That energy had made an outlandish idea into a worldwide movement; taken her all over the globe; and propelled her from one project to the next. I imagined her sitting down and putting a picture or two in the scrapbook, getting distracted by some other idea or person, returning the scrapbook to the closet, and coming back to it hours or days or even months later, to position the next photograph or speech or article that had touched her soul. Looking at that scrapbook, I could feel her energy.

The next one I pulled off the shelf, I had made. Whatever it was that gave her boundless energy, I had that, too. Not like her—I don't know anyone who has her type of energy—but I know I have something that resembles it. I could see it in the way I'd created that book. A picture of Anthony and me with some childhood pals, a baseball card next, an autographed picture of Washington Redskins running back Larry Brown, and then nothing for several pages.

I flipped through the last few leaves, laughing at my lack of attention and follow-though. Until I hit the second-to-last page.

There was a handwritten letter from Dad on legal-sized paper under the plastic covering. I had folded the note at the bottom so it would fit into the eight-by-eleven format.

Happy Graduation Day, Mark, and Congratulations!
Always remember, numero uno, that you are a unique, infinitely valuable person—your Mother & I love you—so do your brothers & sisters & friends—But all our love & interest put together cannot compare with the passionate interest & love God himself showers on you. You are His! He wants <u>you</u>! And He will make you the perfect <u>Man</u> you want to be.
Love, Daddy

It took three or four readings to jog my memory, to get the note to register.

Dad had written the letter the night before I graduated from Georgetown Preparatory School. As he had done before, and as he would do countless times after I graduated, he'd slipped the note under my door sometime during the night, so that when I woke in the morning, the first thing I would see, and read, would be his note.

I don't remember what I did or thought when I got it on that day in May 1982. Nor do I remember putting it in my scrapbook.

Rereading the note all these years later, I smiled at him calling me "numero uno." I know he'd said the same thing to my three brothers, my sister, and my mother—to all six of us, almost every day. But he meant it, to each of us.

He'd believed that I was a unique person. Yes, he'd thought that every person was unique and "infinitely valuable," but to an eighteen-year-old kid trying to figure out who he was, that must have been reassuring. Indeed, I find those four words reassuring today.

Dad didn't write to me on graduation day to tell me that if I worked hard, all my dreams would come true. No, he told me that I was loved by my mom and dad, my siblings and friends, and, most importantly, God—and that love was more important than any other advice or gift he could possibly give.

Since the moment I rediscovered that note in that scrapbook, I have carried it with me in my briefcase and read it every day. Few people nowadays have traditional briefcases, but Dad always carried one. And few people walk around with thirty-year-old letters jammed in their bags, but I can't bear to put the note back in the scrapbook, invisible until, on a rainy, scrapbook-worthy day thirty years from now, I find it again.

Mom and Dad gave me two gifts when I graduated from high school. I was thrilled to get a thirdhand yellow Jeep Wagoneer with eighty-five thousand miles on it, but it broke down on the Massachusetts Turnpike three years later, and I never saw it again. That seventy-three-word sacred note from my guide I see every day now; it's safe in my briefcase, a reminder to keep trying to be as good a man as he.

◇

CHAPTER 39

TRY AND TRY AGAIN

I couldn't believe the three kids and I were already twenty minutes late as we pulled out of the driveway. *Are we ever on time for anything?* I thought. It seemed like we could never get our act together to get out of the house on time when Jeanne wasn't around—and this day she was in Tennessee visiting her mother.

What's more, the trip I had planned to the Shriver homestead had come to mean so much to me; I wanted to show our kids Dad's beginnings, bring his story to them, have them feel that sense of joy I had felt decades before when Dad took me there. And I was running late even for this!

The window in which to visit was short. Already in planning overdrive, I'd figured it all out beforehand. Tommy wanted me to join him in a parent-child tennis tournament scheduled to begin at five. Mass at Our Lady of Mercy started at ten forty-five A.M., which meant that we wouldn't get on the road until noon. Factor in the drive of an hour and thirty minutes, and we wouldn't arrive until close to one-thirty; we would have to leave by three-thirty at the latest to get back in time for the tennis match. That gave us two hours at the most.

So I'd had a great idea: go online to find earlier Masses at churches on the way to the homestead. I'd turned up an eleven A.M. Mass at a church in Damascus, Maryland; that would save us half an hour. I knew we could pull it all off!

As we pulled out of our neighborhood, I handed Molly the monthly missalette that had all the readings for the day's Mass and asked her to read the first and second readings; Tommy would then read the Gospel, and Emma would get the first question. If we were going to be late for Sunday Mass, at least we were going to read the scriptures on the way.

About halfway there, as we discussed the readings, I realized I had forgotten the directions and had only $20 in my wallet. I can't repeat the words I used to describe myself to myself.

We ended up finding the church, but we were thirty minutes late. As the parishioners started singing the final song, I rushed the kids out of the church and we dashed through the parking lot and jumped into the car. We arrived at the homestead at one p.m., giving us two and a half hours before we had to leave.

I parked the car in the big field surrounding the homestead and literally raced the kids across that field to the welcome center. After I purchased the tickets, we ran the forty yards from the gift shop to the old Shriver home. We found two elderly ladies on the front porch in their rockers, waiting for us. I abruptly asked them if they would give us a tour.

The ladies kept rocking. I asked a second time if we could have a tour (you can't go through the home unguided). They looked at each other before one of them groaned, "Well, if you want to have a tour, you have to sit and rock for a while and wait for some more people to show up."

I smiled and told them that we were in a bit of a rush. I

had my agenda, almost as if I had set it in my BlackBerry that morning: tour the house, the gristmill, and the black-smith's shop, then scoot back to Bethesda.

Finally, one lady got up and said, "Okay, I'll take you on the tour."

So we followed her into the homestead. Soon enough, the kids were enthralled—they loved the handmade toys and the 110-year-old wooden sled. Emma's jaw dropped when the tour guide lifted up the blankets to reveal ropes under the mattress of a bed.

The guide asked us, "Does anyone know where the expression 'sleep tight' comes from?" She explained that in the old days, people slept on ropes, and if you wanted a good night's sleep, the ropes needed to be pulled tight before you put your blankets on top of them—hence the expression "sleep tight." The kids loved it.

In the main dining room, I was taken aback by two paintings that used to hang in the front hall of Mom and Dad's house in Potomac. One was of Dad's great-grandmother Mary Owings Shriver, who was born in 1808, and the other was of her husband, William Shriver, born in 1796. She was the mother of thirteen children, including J. E. B. Stuart's scout Thomas Herbert Shriver.

They were serious-looking portraits, plain and simple. When my friends visited my folks, they always found the paintings amusing. Why would a house so filled with laugh-ter and action have two serious-looking old fuddy-duddies in the front hall?

When we sold the house and started giving away some of my parents' "stuff," it was an easy decision to send these paintings of old-time Shrivers to the Union Mills home-stead. Still, seeing them hanging here jolted me. Now they were a part of history.

I gave them one more look and followed the guide into

the kitchen, where we learned how the Shrivers had cooked over a huge fireplace, making all their meals—including their own bread—at home. We walked around the back of the house and saw the privy, an outhouse with three sitting areas. The kids couldn't believe that one!

At the end of the tour, I thanked the woman, and we headed off to the gristmill. The mill is only twenty yards from the main house, but I had the kids trot down the hill to keep things moving along. My mood was halfway between sacred and absurd; the day had gotten ahold of me, it was tugging at my heart, but at the same time I couldn't shake the urge to rush. We couldn't find anyone in the gristmill, so we went over to the barn and had ice cream.

After the kids finished their ice cream, we hurried over to the blacksmith shop. The blacksmith showed us how various metal farming tools were made, and then we hustled over to the gristmill and joined a tour already in progress.

As the tour guide explained how white bread was giving flour a bad name, I kept looking at my watch. The kids seemed interested in the water wheel outside the gristmill and the machinery indoors, but I got the sense that they, too, were getting fidgety. I told them to follow me, and we wandered down the steps to see the machinery below, leaving the rest of the tour group upstairs as the guide kept talking.

Downstairs, Molly said, "Dad, we're going to get in trouble. We left the tour."

"I cannot stand that guy anymore," I said. "He's too long-winded, and we have to move it along. I just wanted to see what's going on down here."

Within two minutes, the tour guide came down the steps, continuing to talk as if nothing had happened. He went over to a corner and moved a lever, which freed water from Big Pipe Creek. The wheel started to turn, which moved the cogs inside the gristmill. Action! Corn was ground on the second floor and we watched as it came down a chute and into a barrel right in front of our eyes. The smell of ground corn filled the room.

The gentleman asked, "Does anyone know where the expression 'keep your nose to the grindstone' comes from?" His question was met with silence, so he proceeded to tell us that when corn is put between two grindstones and ground, if the stones are too close, the corn itself, as a result of the friction, starts to burn. Hence, a good miller literally would put his nose right to the grindstone to ensure that the corn was not being burned.

The tour wrapped up, and we headed to the gift shop, which sold all sorts of memorabilia: Confederate flags reminiscent of the ones displayed before battles in Civil War days, harmonicas like those played by soldiers, flour in little bags. I realized that I had only one dollar left in my wallet and three kids who wanted souvenirs. I ran out of the gift shop and over to the barn to look for Sam Riley, a distant relative who volunteered at the homestead. I found him and asked to borrow $20. Sam smiled, gave me a twenty-dollar bill, and said, "Here you go. Take it."

I asked where I could send him a check. He replied, "Just send a contribution to the homestead and tell them that I lent you the money. It's more important to make a contribution to keep this place going than paying me back. It's great to see you. I hope your kids pick out some nice souvenirs."

I shook his hand and started to trot back to the gift shop.

I stopped dead in my tracks. I felt like Dad had just tapped me on the shoulder.

Here I was, hustling the kids from Bethesda to Damascus

for Mass and then driving as fast as I could to Union Mills and running them through the homestead, all in an effort to hurry back for a tennis match.

What the hell was I doing?

I couldn't believe it—those ladies on their rockers had looked exactly like the woman that Dad had sat down next to when I'd been with him some thirty years earlier. I had missed the opportunity to do with my children exactly what my dad had done with me.

So instead of running into the gift shop, I walked. I handed Molly the twenty. She looked at me quizzically. I told her that she was in charge and to take as long as she needed so that each kid could buy a souvenir. All three kids looked at me kind of funny then, and I said, "Take as much time as you want. We're not going to the tennis match." Tommy said, "We're not going to play, Dad?" I replied, "Not this year, Tommy. We can play when we get home, and if we can't do it today, we'll play tomorrow." He said, "Okay, Dad, no problem. It's a lot of fun here."

I was floored. Tommy didn't really care about the tennis match. I had misjudged, badly.

The kids took their time; Emma and Tommy bought harmonicas, and Molly bought cornmeal. What we were going to do with those harmonicas and cornmeal, God alone knows, but they had their memories of Union Mills, and that was what mattered.

As we ambled to the parking lot, we saw a bunch of antique cars parked there to entertain the crowd. We got into the back seat of a Model T and had our picture taken by the owner. I looked out beyond the cars, at the big field that rolled away from the homestead. There were two handsome mules giving rides to kids and, off in the distance, a couple of families having a picnic.

Instead of barreling down the highway, we went to visit my grandparents' grave site in downtown Westminster, seven miles away. Dad's only sibling, Herbert, is also buried there, alongside his wife, Willa. About a month earlier, I'd received a bill from the cemetery, asking for a yearly maintenance payment. I'd called the office and asked, "What's the fee for?"

"Your father planted hedges all around the cemetery years ago," the manager had said, "in honor of your grandparents and his brother and his sister-in-law. We maintain it all year long, and your dad paid the bill."

My kids and I walked through the graveyard and found the Shriver burial plot. It's pretty easy to find—Dad had commissioned a huge concrete cross with SHRIVER in capital letters to mark the location. I showed the kids the wooden cross Dad had encased in the larger concrete cross, the one that had lain on President Kennedy's casket and had been blessed by the pope and the patriarch, and told them the whole story. They listened intently.

We got back into our car and drove the hour and a half home, but not before stopping at McDonald's—which, despite my kids' fondness for the french fries, we don't do often.

Jeanne arrived home later that evening. When she asked the kids what they had done, their responses came fast and furious. Emma described the old toys in detail; Molly jumped in and explained the expression "sleep tight"; and Tommy recounted the mechanics of the gristmill. They talked about the gift shop and the antique cars, the ice cream and Big Pipe Creek. They even spoke about the cemetery and the cross. As I listened to them talk, I saw myself at their age, after the same trip so many years ago with Dad, feeling the mystery and excitement that that place, and Dad's story, can elicit.

◇

That night, after the kids had gone to sleep, I wandered downstairs to the basement and stared at the cinder blocks.

How the hell did you do it all, Dad? You made the trips to the homestead so fun and exciting and interesting. You played sports with us, you made us laugh and smile. All the while, you were working to help people, creating new programs, opening the doors of opportunity to millions, but you never forgot your wife and kids. How did you balance it? I screwed up the trip to the homestead until the very end, and God knows I don't have as much on my mind as you did.

I wish I could have just one more conversation with you, ask you how you did it—and how you were so alive, so joyful, yet so looking forward to meeting God, so happy during your time on this earth and so zealous for the life after. Is it really that hard, Dad? Does a husband, a father today have more expectations on the home front than you did? Is that the reason that it's so hard, or do we—do I—just complicate life by adding too much to my plate and end up losing track of it all?

But I can't call you, I can't speak with you—all I have left are your stories, your letters, your speeches.

On my desk sat President Clinton's eulogy; I reread it. He had spoken after we five siblings had given our remarks. He'd addressed what I imagine everyone in the church was thinking at that point in time.

"I had the opportunity to observe him in two settings," President Clinton said, "which answered a question that even in the most hopeful times was hard to answer with a straight face: could anybody really be as good as he seemed to be?" The audience started to laugh. Then he said, "I mean, come on now! This is, like, come on! Every other man in this church feels about two inches tall right now."

The audience roared, and more than anything, I felt grateful. I had had a father whose shoes I could never fill, against whom I would never measure up, yet I felt no pressure to do so.

I read some more of Clinton's eulogy:

He knew that what mattered is the moment and eternity, and most of us waste countless hours trying to rewrite the past or elevate our position in the future in a way that doesn't amount to a hill of beans and keeps us from making the most of a moment. I have never met a man in my life who was happier in the moment than Sargent Shriver, and who made more of it and who thought less about how he could rewrite the past or reach into the future to inflate himself above others.

So I tell you, from the cynical tough times of the late sixties and early seventies to this amazing moment, he really was as good as his family just told you, and maybe even a little better, and a whole generation of us understood what President Kennedy meant by looking at Sargent Shriver's life.

I paused at that line: "A whole generation of us understood what President Kennedy meant by looking at Sargent Shriver's life."

Was I was any closer to understanding Sargent Shriver's life? I'd thought I'd come to understand his life better and had learned from him, but then I'd screwed up the trip to the homestead . . . saving the day only at the very end.

My eyes wandered past the kids' drawings and watercolors on the wall, past the pictures of Jeanne, and settled on a box not five feet from me. It was jammed with Mass cards and the programs from Mom's and Dad's funerals. I picked up one of Dad's programs and opened it. On the inside flap was a picture of Mom and Dad at a table. In it, Mom is smiling a big toothy grin while Dad, eyes closed tight, is kissing her cheek like there is no tomorrow. There's a bottle of champagne on the table and a small American flag. They were young and happy and having a party, and their vitality—even though I'd experienced it every day of my life—was still startling to behold.

I turned the page. The Mass program was next, then the *Baltimore Catechism* quote, accompanied by pictures of Dad as a baby and a young boy.

Then a wedding shot—God, did they look happy!

I flipped through the rest of the thirteen-page program and closed it.

On the back cover was a statement—a testament, I suppose—written by Dad when he was eighty-seven years old:

I am a man who was born and has tried to live committed to being open to all people, no matter their differences in nationality, race, religion, or geography.

I am a man who is full of energy and health.

I am a man who takes his responsibilities seriously. I am committed to doing everything I can to succeed.

I am a man who is original and creative.

I am a man who is unencumbered by the past and by existing hierarchies.

I feel free to invent.

I believe the world was and is created by God. I believe the world is good beyond description.

I believe that we human beings who seek life, liberty, and the pursuit of happiness do so because God has given us these things. They are a gift.

I believe that we have a responsibility to God to do whatever we can to do good things for people, especially the poor.

I believe in ideals. I believe that the world can be better if only we focus on achieving our ideals.

I believe that any failure to achieve our ideals should only result in a rededication to them.

I believe in faith, hope, and love. I believe that they have power.

Enough said. Good night, good man.

ACKNOWLEDGMENTS

W hen one of my college roommates, Dick Burke, heard that I was writing this book, he called me and said, "How are you going to write a book on your dad? He wrote everything you ever claimed to have written!"

As usual, Dick had it almost right. Dad was my best editor, and I was terrified at the prospect of writing a book without his help. I had no idea, though, how many people would help me, people who, I know, did so because they loved—yes, loved—Dad. I felt that love time and again.

Another college roommate, Paul Hardart, encouraged me countless times to write this story. He wrote me encouraging e-mails; when I visited him in New York City, our dinner conversation soon turned to the book, and again he encouraged me to write. He even developed an outline for the book based on my eulogy and his own relationship with Dad. He edited drafts, added words and ideas, and always offered encouragement. Paul and I met in the fall of our freshman year at Holy Cross, and I can't imagine a more loyal, dedicated friend. I would not have written this book without Paul's persistence.

Paul also introduced me to Greg Jordan, a writer from Baltimore, who worked alongside me every step of the way.

Greg's questions pulled stories out of me that I had long forgotten; his words, ideas, and edits have made this book much stronger. His presence, both physically and emotionally, spurred me to work harder. Greg never met my father, but after working on this book with me for five months, he told me one day that he was going to ask his girlfriend to marry him. I congratulated him and asked what moved him to make the decision.

"It was your father," he said. "Throughout this process, I've come to see your dad as a good friend of mine. I felt him telling me to make a commitment to marriage, make a commitment to love."

I couldn't have been happier for Ali and Greg—and for Dad for making new friends!

I am grateful that Donald Cardinal Wuerl, Archbishop of Washington, invited Father Bill Byrne and me to dinner about six weeks after Dad's funeral. When I mentioned the book idea, they encouraged me to write. Their timing was perfect; their words were the final push I needed.

My cousin Caroline Kennedy taught me the ropes of the publishing business. Her words of encouragement, and her sense of humor, were invaluable.

When my memory was cloudy, I relied on Jeannie Main, Dad's loyal longtime assistant, to clear things up. She has an almost encyclopedic memory, and if she was unsure, she knew exactly whom to call or how to get the answer. She is amazing.

Scott Stossel's exceptional biography of my father, *Sarge: The Life and Times of Sargent Shriver*, was enormously helpful not only in its detailed account of my dad's life but in pointing me toward sources I might otherwise not have known. Whenever I was confused about something, Scott always called me back immediately and set the record straight. Dad had many blessings in his life; finding as talented a writer to pen his biography was a blessing for all the Shrivers.

Harris Wofford told me story after story of Dad's life many years ago, parts of which I have included in this book and all of which I will never forget.

Jane Sewell and James Shriver III provided insight into the history of the Shriver homestead. Their warmth and passion for history have made me even prouder to be a Shriver and a Marylander.

Tom Songster and Dicken Yung provided details on Dad's trip to China on behalf of Special Olympics, and Helen MacNabb and Kirsten Seckler were extremely helpful on all things Special Olympics.

Elaine Ragsdale told me stories that I never knew about Dad and Rags's relationship. I am forever grateful for her help—and, more important, for sharing her husband with us for so many years.

Phil Lee and Jonathan Weinberg told me stories about Dad and my campaigns that I had never heard; their friendship means so much to me. John Bouman, the president of the Sargent Shriver National Center on Poverty Law, explained the funding history of Legal Services. He is a role model of whom Dad would be so proud.

Vicki Kennedy told me the wonderful story of sailing on the Mya, and she clarified the difference between a schooner and a sloop—a conversation I'll never forget!

Dad and Mom had great medical care, especially during the last few years of their lives. Dr. Beth Horowitz and Dr. Roy Fried led those efforts; for their medical help and for their help with the myriad of health issues discussed in this book, I remain in their debt.

Scott Tracy and Hilary Stephens helped clarify details of the funeral. They are good friends to the Shrivers.

My bosses at Save the Children, Charlie MacCormack and Carolyn Miles, gave me time to write, and Kathy Spangler picked up the slack in my absence. I am grateful for their help and support. Save the Children board members Bill Haber and Tom Murphy gave me sage advice throughout the process; they also made me laugh and keep it all in perspective. I am blessed to have two such wonderful mentors in my life.

Jonathan Capehart helped design the book jacket, as did Janet and Paul Nolan and their two children, Connor and Meredith. Steve Davenport at the Library of Congress not only found the *True Magazine* article from 1965 that I quoted, but he lent me two dollars to copy it. I met him that morning—talk about a true public servant!

Herve Humler was my expert translator, helping with French spelling and grammar.

Special thanks to President Clinton for allowing me to quote from his eulogy. Ana Maria Coronel on his staff was a tremendous help in making that happen. I am extremely grateful to U2 for allowing me to quote from "Beautiful Day." Sharon Callaly and Paul McGuinness secured that permission in record time.

Finding pictures for the book was a surprisingly challenging task. Laurie Austin, Chris Banks, Karen Chaput, Carolyn Gleason, Cathy Hardman, Teri Hess, Larry Levin, Kate McKenna, Tom McNaught, Stacy Rhodes, Matthew Sheaff, Sandra Wareing, Christina Wiginton and Mark Wylie all pitched in to help, and Coral Collins and Doug Klein searched high and low for historic photos of the homestead.

I relied heavily on the edits and ideas of a group of people that I am blessed to call friends: My oldest pal, Tony Williams, sent edits while he flew across the country. Bruce Stewart, another college roommate, and his wife, Lauretta, also a Holy Cross graduate and a pal for thirty years, gave me a double-barreled critique. They had great ideas, and I will never forget their enthusiasm for this book, and their love of Dad. Neil Grauer, an accomplished author, offered brilliant criticisms and wonderful pictures for the book; Jamie Price made the Peace Corps section richer. My hunting buddy and campaign manager, Steve Neill, made the introduction more vivid. Father Bill English and Father Richard Fragomeni provided constructive criticism and words of support. Rob Granader moved to England for a year, but that didn't stop him from checking in constantly and offering his sound advice on the draft. Tim Maloney knows more about Maryland history and politics than anyone alive; I appreciate his help on that section. Dr. Charles Steinberg knows more about the Baltimore Orioles than anyone else. He was my boss when I interned with the O's in 1982, and he has remained a good friend. I am grateful for his edits on all things baseball. Tim Hanlon took the draft on his Christmas vacation and his e-mail critique was the first one in my inbox in 2012. Brad Blank allowed me to use the fax machine at his summer rental in Hyannis Port. For that alone, I am grateful; his edits and his more than forty years of friendship are icing on the cake.

I met Nick Galifianakis at a cocktail party and called him three days later to ask if he would read the book. He did and his comments made the story much stronger. John Tydings offered sage advice when I was struggling with competing priorities; I am grateful for his counsel and friendship.

Dad's longtime friend, the great writer and peace activist Colman McCarthy, offered what he called "some weeding, some pruning"; I have saved his edits, they are so brilliant.

My agent, David Kuhn, made the proposal much, much stronger. I am grateful for that and for steering me through the entire process. Billy Kingsland in David's office was always available and very helpful. Bob Corcoran and Bill

Josephson gave me great legal advice, as they did for Dad for decades. How lucky for us both! Steven Fisher has a gift for strategic public relations. I am glad that we work together.

The team at Holt was wonderful—when I met Steve Rubin, I immediately liked him. He has a first-rate team in Pat Eisemann, Maggie Richards, Maggie Sivon, Kenn Russell, and Allison Adler. They, in turn, introduced me to their excellent copy editor, Bonnie Thompson, whom I wish I had known while I was in college. And Sam Bayard is the clearest-talking lawyer I have ever worked with. What a collection of talent! Steve should give them all a big pay raise.

This book, though, would never have materialized without the brilliance of my editor at Holt, Gillian Blake. She restructured the book, edited it, and then reread and edited it countless times. She listened intently to my ideas about the book cover and layout design; she agreed with some ideas and had good reasons why others wouldn't work. She patiently answered every question I had, and I had a lot of them! She was relentless and insightful, funny and warm. That's a hard combination to come by. She is a gem.

Betsy Zorio, my assistant for the last six years, worked on the manuscript early in the morning and late at night, on weekends, and while she was on vacation. She made edits, caught mistakes, and found answers to my questions. To say that she is multitalented sells her skills short. She told me at the outset of this endeavor that because of Dad it was "an honor" to work on the project; it was my honor to work with her.

Finally, my family. My sisters-in-law, Malissa, Linda, and Alina, offered words of encouragement and support, and Alina helped find pictures and design the book jacket. She has a great eye—I am still struggling to see what she sees in Anthony, however!

Bobby, Maria, Timmy, and Anthony couldn't have been more supportive, sharing stories that I hadn't heard, and offering changes to the text. I am the fifth-best writer in this fivesome—I love each of them and am grateful that they helped me so.

Molly, Tommy, and Emma provided love and inspiration throughout this process. As I looked at them every day that I wrote, they revealed insights into my dad that I had failed to see. And they kept me laughing at times when I was sad—my favorite line belongs to Molly, who told me one day that she was going to write a book about me.

"Thank you, honey," I said. "That is so sweet."

She paused and said, "I think I'll call it *An OK Dad*."

And to my best friend, the person who edited my eulogy for Dad, who read every draft and every word of this book and made it better, who gave me the space to write and the love and support to keep at it, who makes me smile and laugh every day—to Jeanne, I say, simply, thank you.

You are the best and I love you.

Happy Graduation Day,

Mark, + Congratulations!

Always remember, numero
uno, that you are a unique,
infinitely valuable person —
Your Mother + I love
you — So do your brothers +
sisters + friends — But all
our love + interest put
together cannot compare
with the passionate interest +
love God himself showers on
you. You are His! He wants
you! And He will make
you the perfect Man you
want to be. Love, Daddy

ABOUT THE AUTHOR

MARK K. SHRIVER is the senior vice president of U.S. Programs at Save the Children in Washington, D.C. Shriver created the Choice Program, served in the Maryland state legislature for eight years, and served as chair of the National Commission on Children and Disasters. He lives with his wife, Jeanne, and their three children, Molly, Tommy, and Emma, in Maryland.